MUSIC IN MOTION

Originated by: MICHAEL DAVID WOJCIO
Developed by: GERILEE GUSTASON
ESTHER ZAWOLKOW
Illustrated by: CAROLYN NORRIS

Modern Signs Press, Inc.

Los Alamitos, California

Modern Signs Press, Inc.
P.O. Box 1181
Los Alamitos, CA 90720
(562) 596-8548 (Voice or TTY)
FAX (562) 795-6614
Email modsigns@aol.com
website www.modernsignspress.com

The publisher welcomes your comments and suggestions on this and future editions.

ISBN No. 0-916708-07-1

Printed in the United States of America

TABLE OF CONTENTS

INTRODUCTION

The deaf and hard-of-hearing often use their hands to communicate. The hearing may also use their hands to help facilitate communication. A mime can make an audience imagine a wall in front of him, and anyone can use gestures to enhance speech. Consequently, everyone sometimes puts their hands in motion to talk, entertain, or help convey a message. A beautiful medium to complement motion is through music.

Music has always been one of the most popular forms of entertainment. Many lyricists, composers, and singers have become famous by delighting people with two things–good lyrics and a complementary melody line. There is a third ingredient that can give songs even more life. That ingredient is sign language. Deaf and hard-of-hearing children and adults can appreciate songs with these three ingredients and enjoy signing them. Sign language can also be used as a way for the hearing to learn the artistry of meaningful movement through song. We put another dimension in music by signing songs, and therefore will become more involved with every song that we sign.

Several years ago, I found it very enjoyable signing songs to a hard-of-hearing boy at Starr King Exceptional School in Carmichael, California. This led to my master's project entitled "Signing Words Through Songs As A Tool For Teaching Dactylology To Elementary School Children" at California State University in Sacramento. Using the following procedure, I taught five hearing children (seven to ten years old) eight songs: First I taught them the manual alphabet. Then we signed eight children's songs and arranged all the words in alphabetical order. One child who was learning disabled had learned 40 signs; the other children learned between 110 and 140 signs.

Selecting songs for this book was very difficult because of the vast number of verses that have been written. We had to consider songs on the basis of tempo, lyrics, and (for the most part) popularity. Most of the songs we chose are relatively slow.

What value does a children's sign book have for the public? It will promote sign language and help bridge the gap between the deaf and hearing world. How should anyone proceed when learning the signs? One must follow the first step as indicated in my master's project - learn the manual alphabet that is illustrated in **Music in Motion**. This will facilitate signing the songs. We hope that this will arouse your interest so that you will want to learn more Signing Exact English signs and other systems like Visual English, American Sign Language, and others. Similarly, this signed song book will enhance many sign language courses and be a wonderful form of entertainment at home.

One December I signed a holiday song at an auditorium engagement at Hartshorn Elementary School in Short Hills, New Jersey. Even though most of the children never signed before, many were able to follow my hands. One teacher told me that she had tears in her eyes and felt the song more that ever before. We have reached a new horizon. Let us explore it.

Michael David Wojcio

EXPLANATION OF SIGN PICTURES AND DESCRIPTIONS

Each word of each song has a drawing of a manual sign representing that word. In the glossary at the back of the book is a written description of how the sign is made. This description is for the basic sign. Sometimes the picture varies to illustrate a possible variation in sign production that can add to the interpretation of the song. For instance, in "The Magic Penny" away is signed with the right hand the first time. the left hand the second time, and both hands the third time. Signs may be made where the object would be seen; for example, bow in "Sing a Rainbow" is made overhead. Similarly, the eyes should look in the direction of the object – as in the upward gaze in "Twinkle, Twinkle, Little Star" or when speaking of the snow coming down in "Winter Day." Use of such variations and facial expression can add a great deal to a song's signed interpretation.

Suffixes(-s, -ing, etc.) are represented in smaller pictures to the right of the basic sign. They should be signed smoothly as part of the same work, and not as a separate word. Be guided by the flow of speech, and sign smoothly, gliding from one word into another.

Enjoy this experience of signing songs!

Twinkle, Twinkle, Little Star

Oh Where, Oh Where
Has My Little Dog Gone?

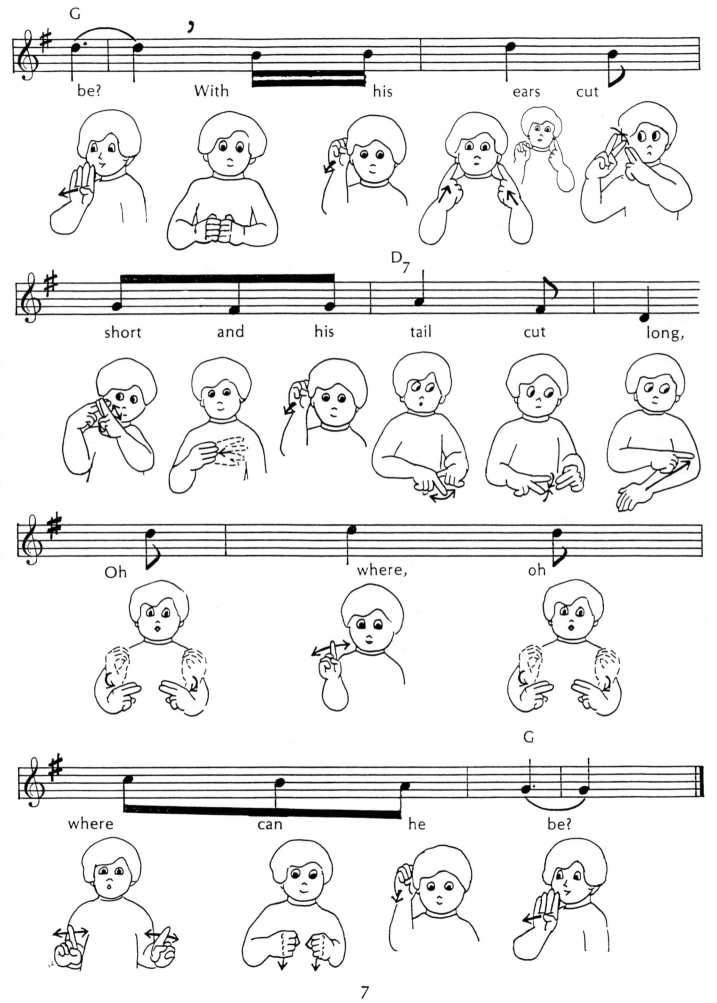

be? With his ears cut

short and his tail cut long,

Oh where, oh

where can he be?

Place To Be

Words and Music by Malvina Reynolds

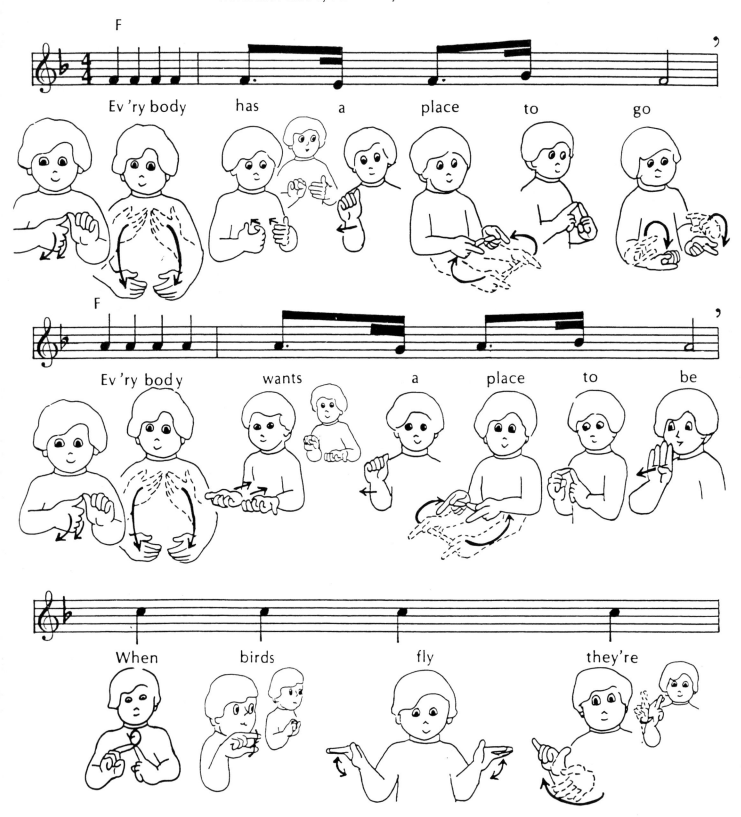

swimming in the sky. while

fish are swim — ming in the sea.

Ev — 'ry bod — y has a place to go

Ev _ 'ry _ bod ___ y wants to be somewhere

Lob ___ sters live at the

bottom of the sea while I'm

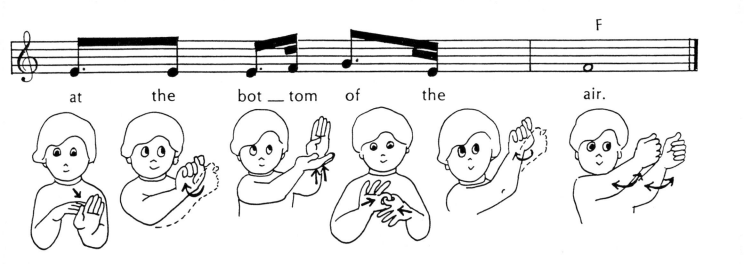

at the bot __ tom of the   air.

My Hat It Has Three Corners

Lyrics and melody of "My Hat It Has Three Corners" from WHAT SHALL WE DO AND ALLEE GALLOO!
collected and edited by Marie Winn, musical arrangement by Allan Miller.

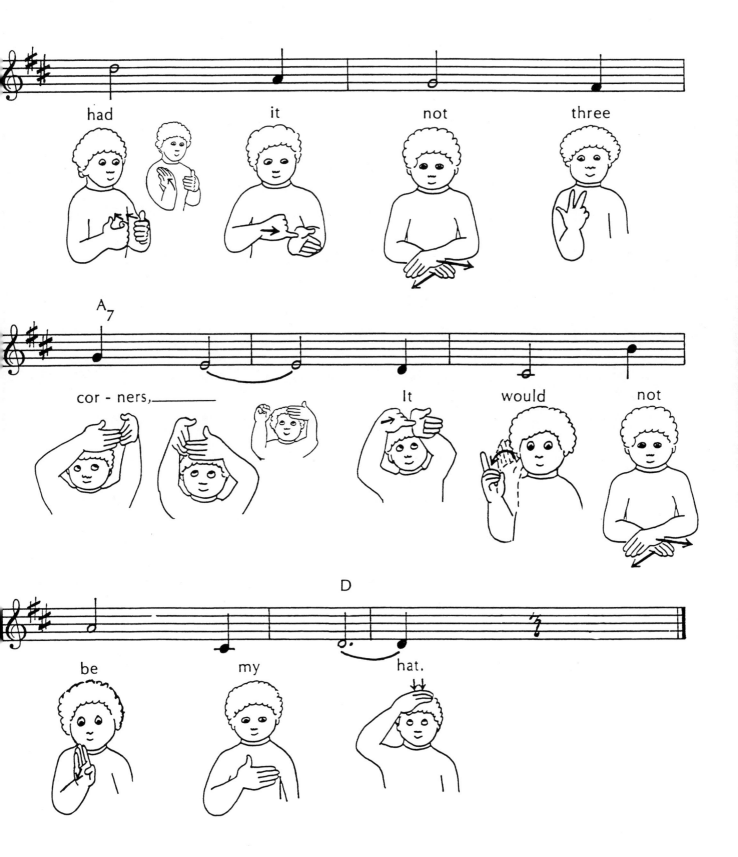

had   it   not   three

cor - ners,_____   It   would   not

be   my   hat.

Happy Birthday To You

by Mildred Hill

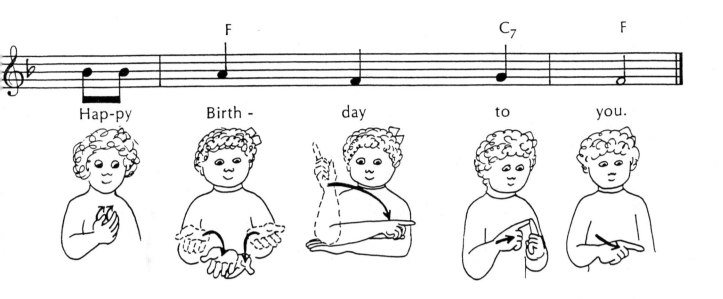

Hap-py   Birth -   day   to   you.

NAME-SIGN   Tap the left shoulder with the right hand in the letter of the first letter of the desired name— "L" for Linda, "C" for Craig, etc.

15

Who Has The Ring?

From SILVER BURDETT MUSIC 3

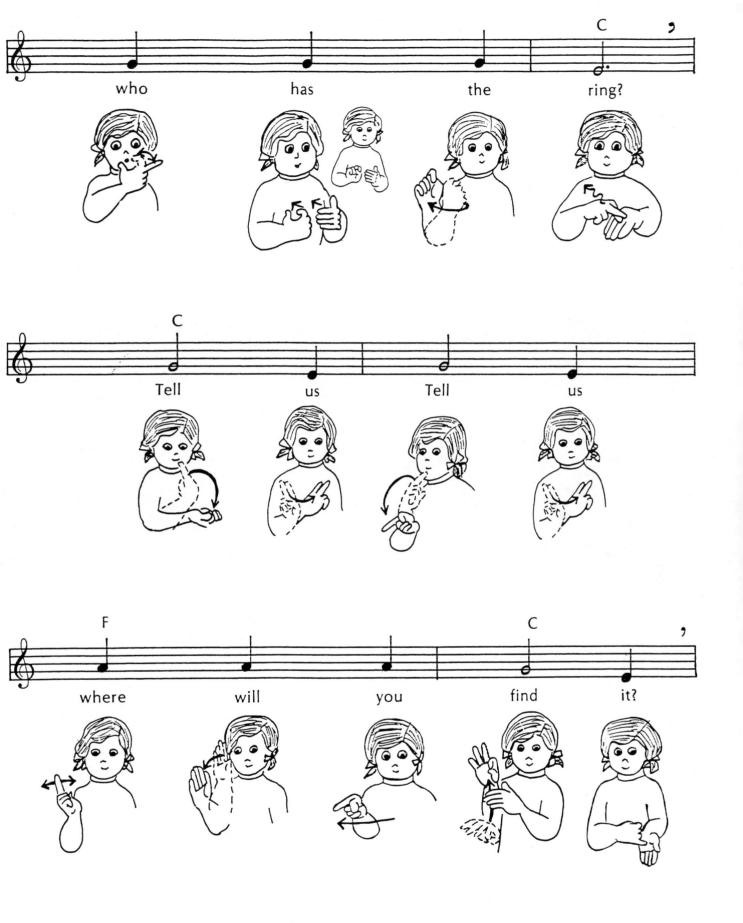

NAME-SIGN   Tap the left shoulder with the right hand in the letter of the first letter of the desired name—"L" for Linda, "C", for Craig, etc.

18

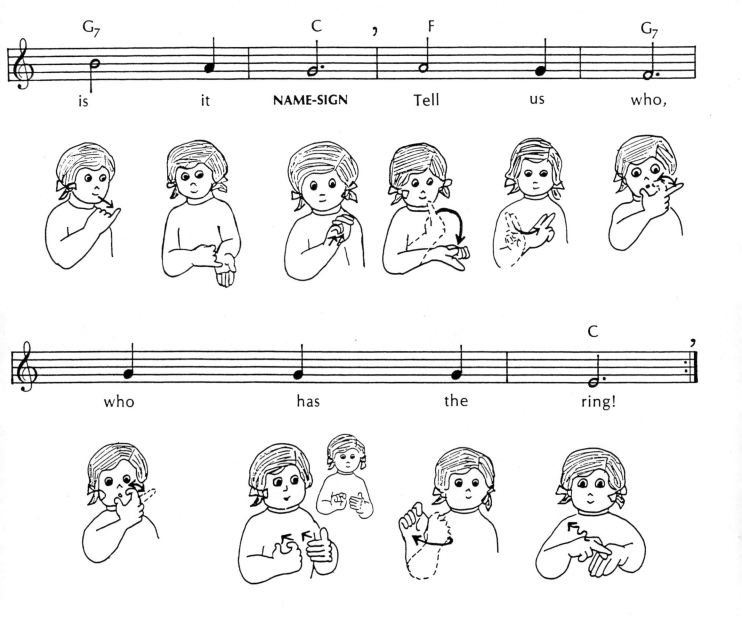

Let's Go Walking

Lyrics and melody of "Let's Go Walking" from ANOTHER SINGING TIME:
Songs for Nursery & School by Satis N. Coleman and Alice G. Thorn.

Run, Run, Run

Words & Music by Christopher Dedrick

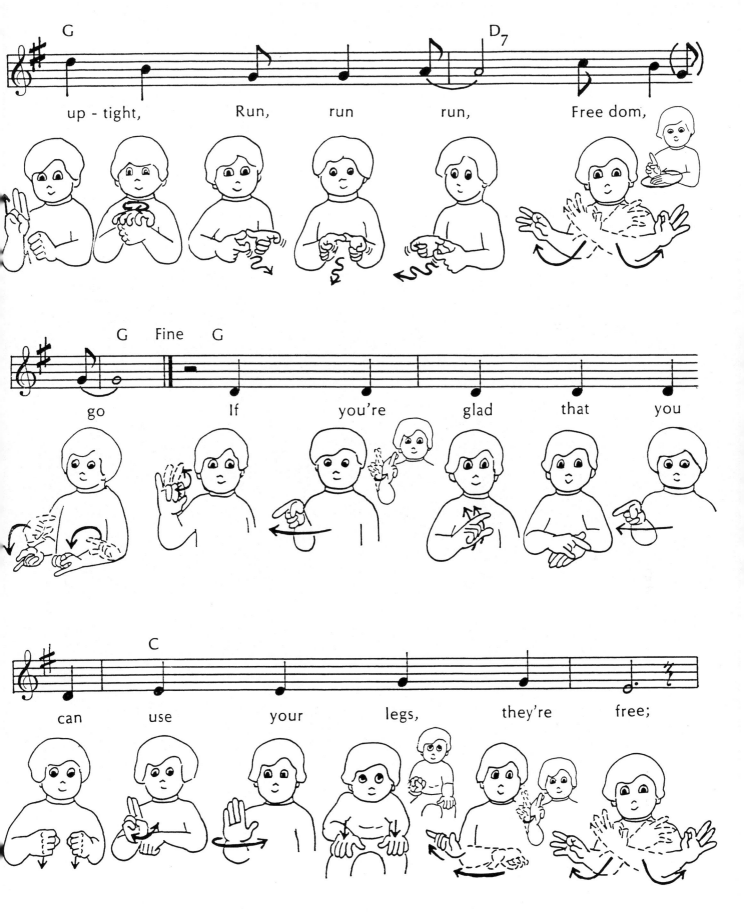

if you're glad that you can

use your eyes to see,

If you're glad the world has

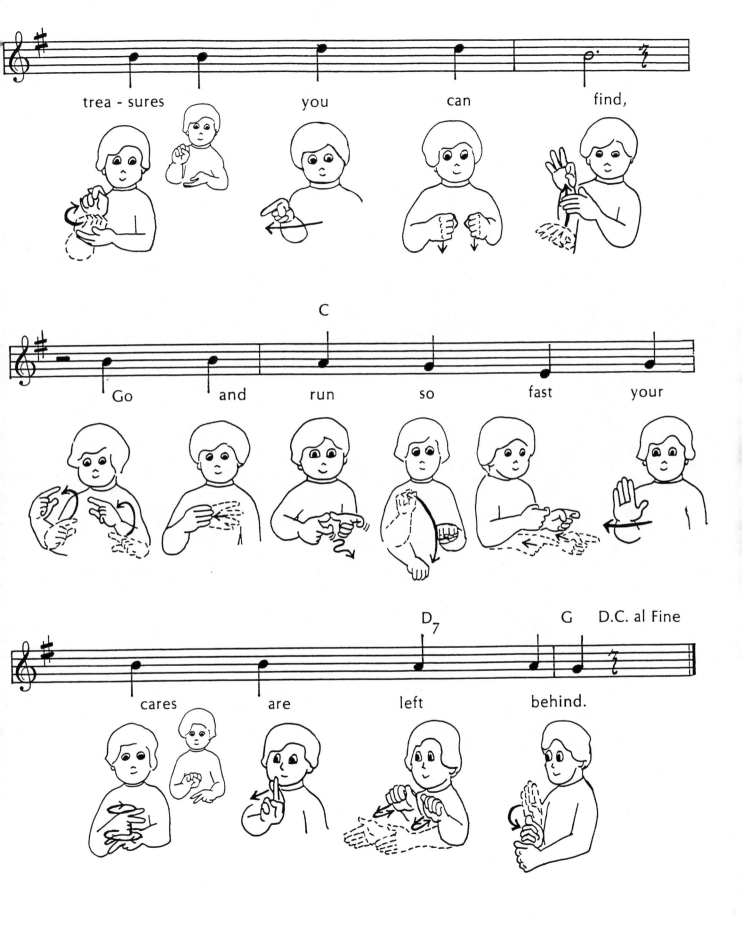

trea - sures you can find,

C

Go and run so fast your

D₇ G D.C. al Fine

cares are left behind.

Magic Penny

Words and Music by Malvina Reynolds

if you give it a - way,—

(B7)   B7   E   Fine

You end up hav - ing more.

A   E

It's just like a mag - ic pen - ny,

27

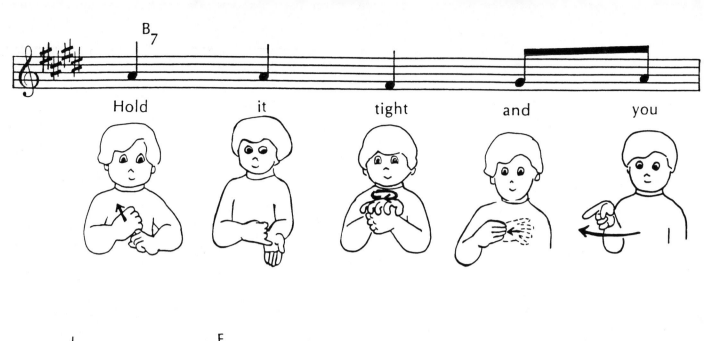

Hold   it   tight   and   you

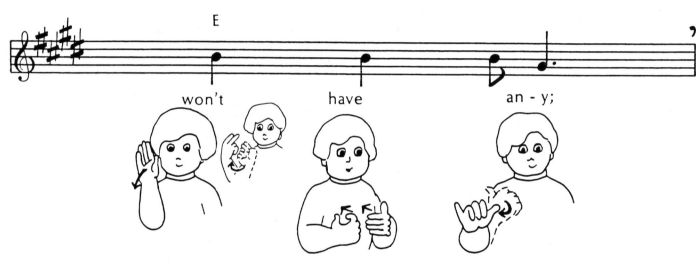

won't   have   an - y;

Lend   it;   spend__   it,   and   you'll

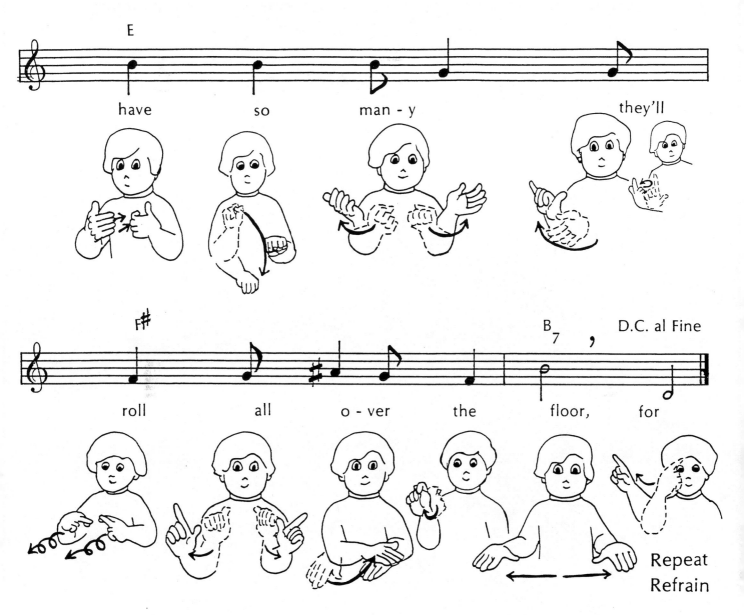

Little Things

Words by Julia A. Fletcher

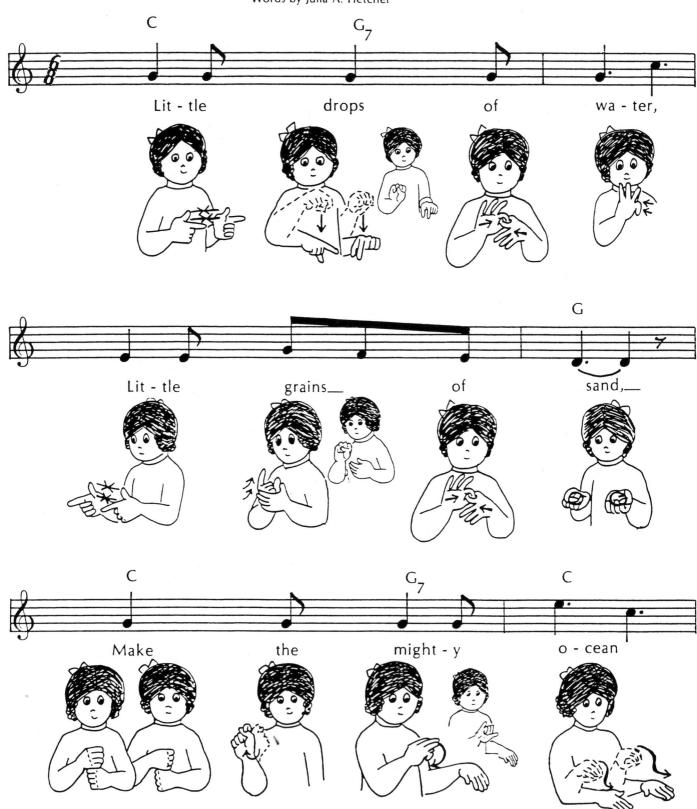

From GROWING WITH MUSIC. Wilson et al., Book 1 (Englewood Cliffs, NJ: Prentice-Hall, Inc., 1966)

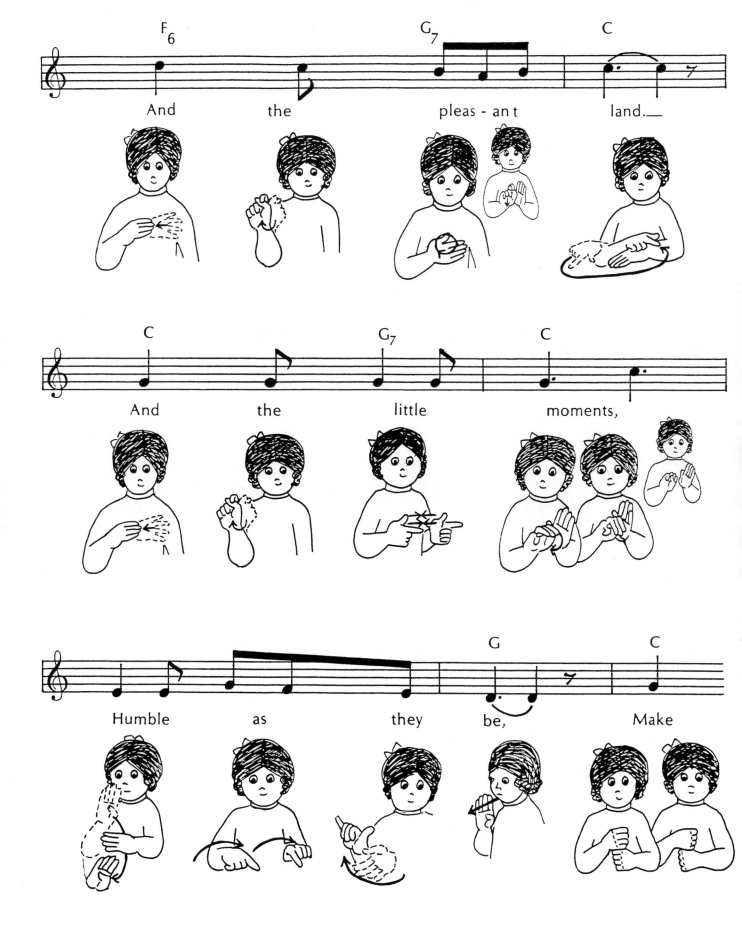

the mighty ages Of eternity.

Little deeds of kindness,

Little words of love,

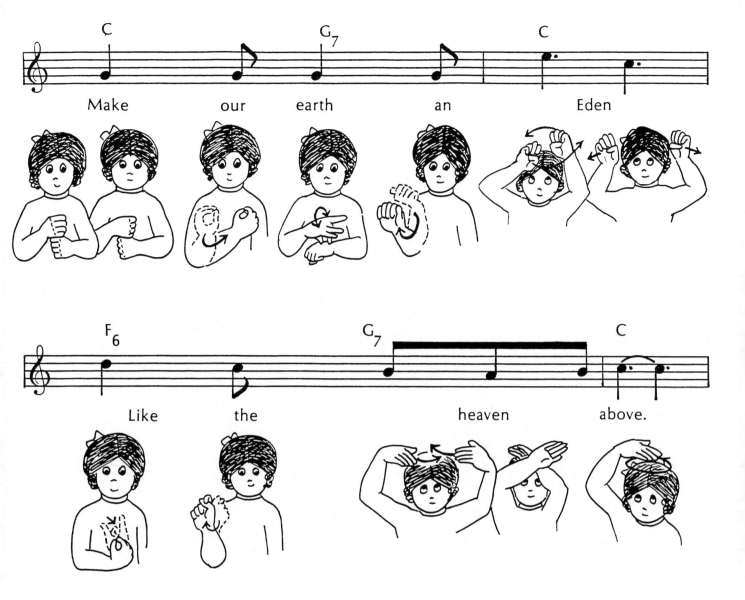

The Seasons

Words and Music by Joan Haines

From GROWING WITH MUSIC. Wilson et al., Book 2 (Englewood Cliffs, NJ: Prentice-Hall, Inc., 1966).

34

make   up   a   year,

Sing   them   by   col - or   and

sing   them   by   name.

Sing A Rainbow

Words and Music by Arthur Hamilton

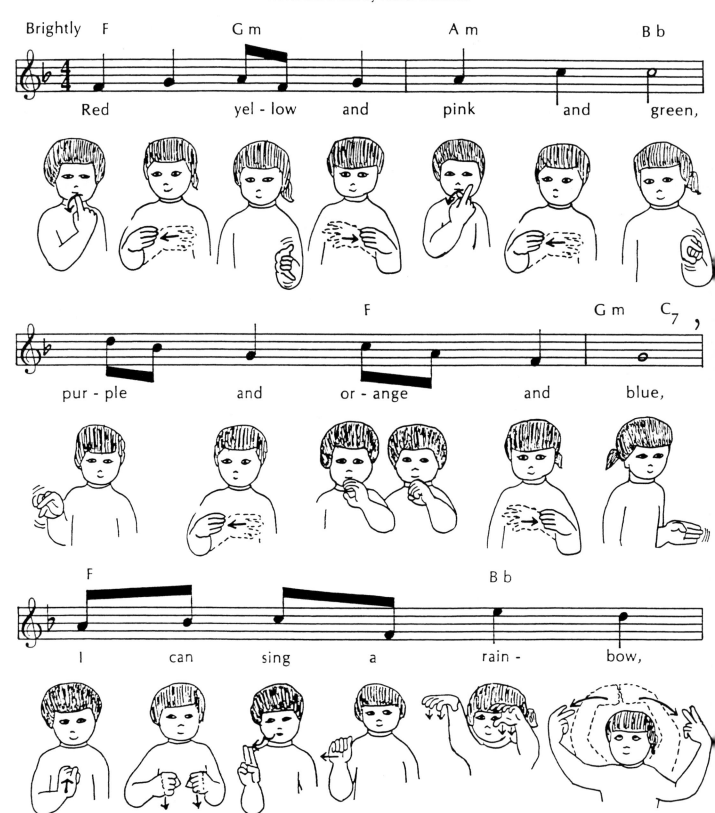

sing a rain - bow,

sing a rain - bow, too.

Lis-ten with your eyes;

lis-ten with your eyes and

sing ev-'ry- thing you see.

You can sing a rain- bow,

38

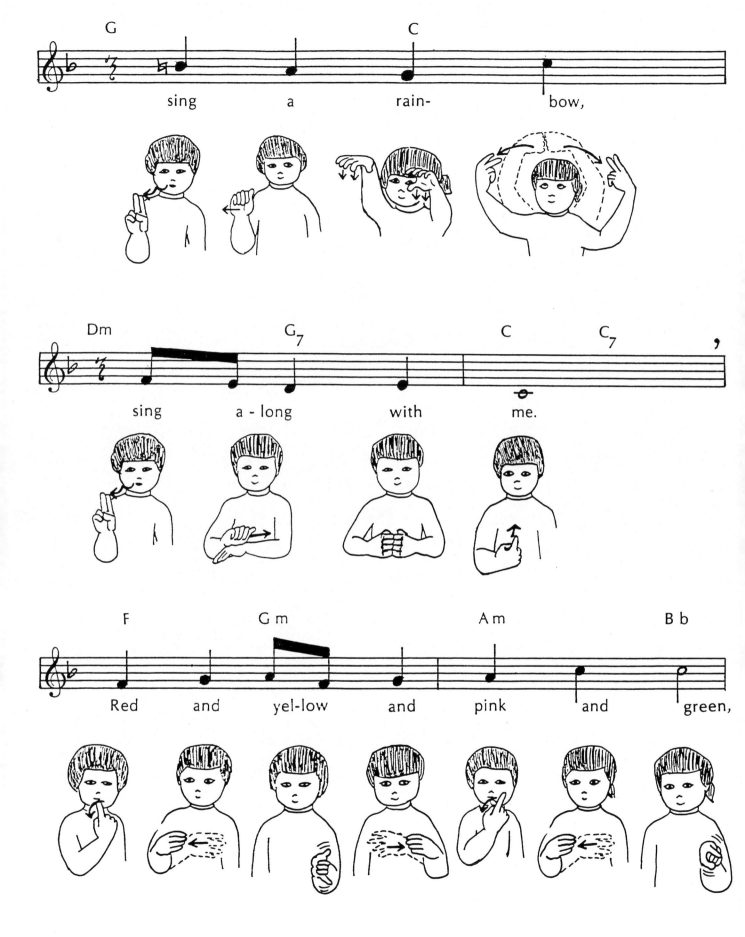

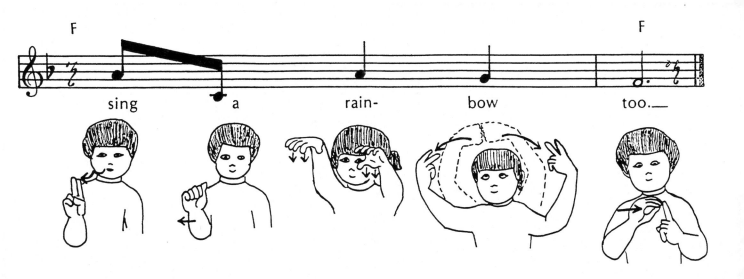

sing   a   rain-   bow   too.___

Raindrops

from THE SMALL SINGER by Lucille Wood and Roberta McLaughlin

One lit - tle rain - drop

rid - ing on a cloud,

Rid - ing on a cloud,

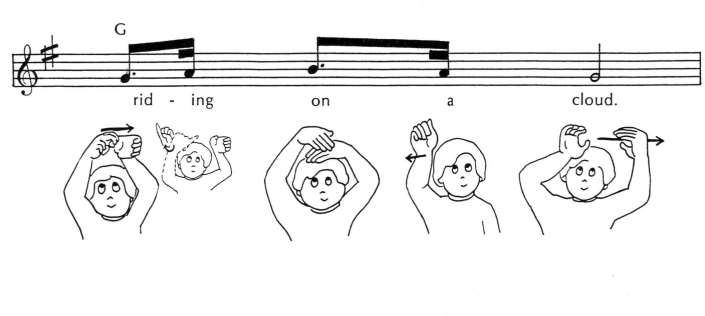

rid - ing on a cloud.

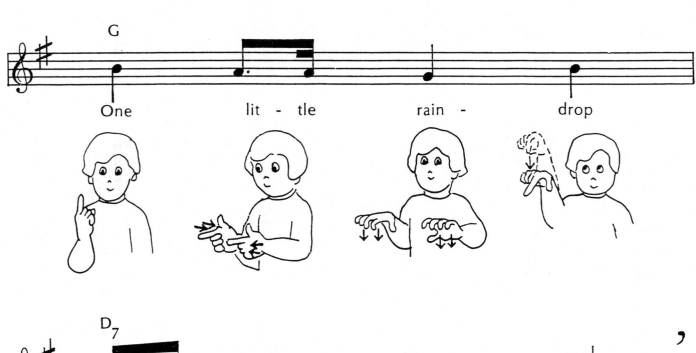

One lit - tle rain - drop

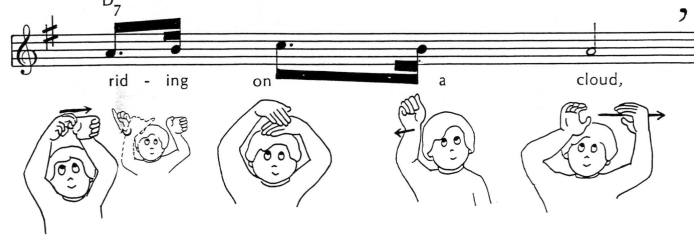

rid - ing on a cloud,

43

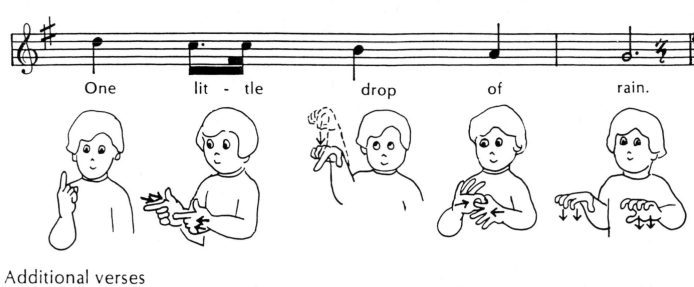

One lit - tle drop of rain.

Additional verses

Verse 2.

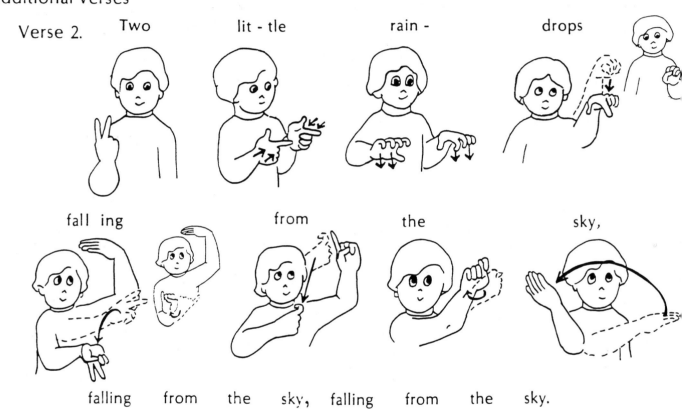

Two lit - tle rain - drops

fall ing from the sky,

falling from the sky, falling from the sky.
Two little raindrops falling from the sky,

Two lit - tle drops of rain.

44

Verse 3. Three   little   rain   drops

knocking   on   the   roof,

knocking   on   the   roof,   knocking   on   the   roof.
Three   little   raindrops   knocking   on   the   roof,
Three   little   drops   of   rain.

Verse 4. Four   little   rain   drops

dancing   up   and   down,

dancing   up   and   down,   dancing   up   and   down.
Four   little   raindrops   dancing   up   and   down,
Four   little   drops   of   rain.

Verse 5.   Five   little   rain   drops

sliding   down   the   pane,

sliding   down   the   pane,   sliding   down   the   pane.
Five   little   raindrops   sliding   down   the   pane,
Five   little   drops   of   rain

Verse

6.   Six   little   rain   drops   sleeping

in   the   sun,

sleeping   in   the   sun,   sleeping   in   the   sun.
Six   little   raindrops   sleeping   in   the   sun,
Six   little   drops   of   rain

46

Verse 7.
Seven   little   rain   drops

run   away   and   hide,

run   away   and   hide,   run   away   and   hide.
Seven   little   raindrops   run   away   and   hide,
Seven   little   drops   of   rain.

47

On A Winter Day

from RHYTHMS TO READING by Lucille Wood

On   a   win - ter   day.___

Additional verses   Verse 2.

This   is   the   way   it   cov - ers   the   town,

cov - ers   the   town,   cov - ers   the   town,

This   is   the   way   it   cov - ers

the   town,   On   a   win - ter   day.___

Verse 3.

This   is   the   way   the

cold   winds   blow

cold   winds   blow

cold   winds   blow

This   is   the   way   the

cold   winds   blow

on   a   winter   day

50

Verse 4.

This   is   the   way   we

shovel   the   snow,

shovel   the   snow

shovel   the   snow

This   is   the   way   we

shovel   the   snow

on   a   winter   day

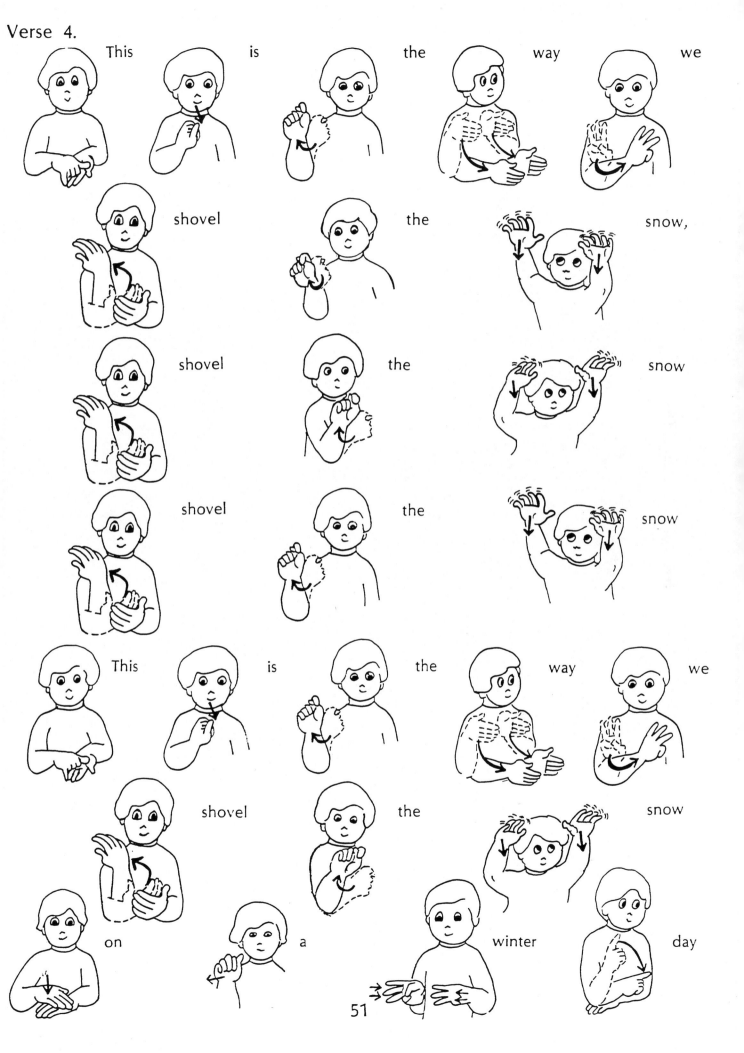

51

Verse 5.

This   is   the   way   we

roll   the   snow,

roll   the   snow

roll   the   snow

This   is   the   way   we

roll   the   snow

on   a   winter   day

52

Verses 6.

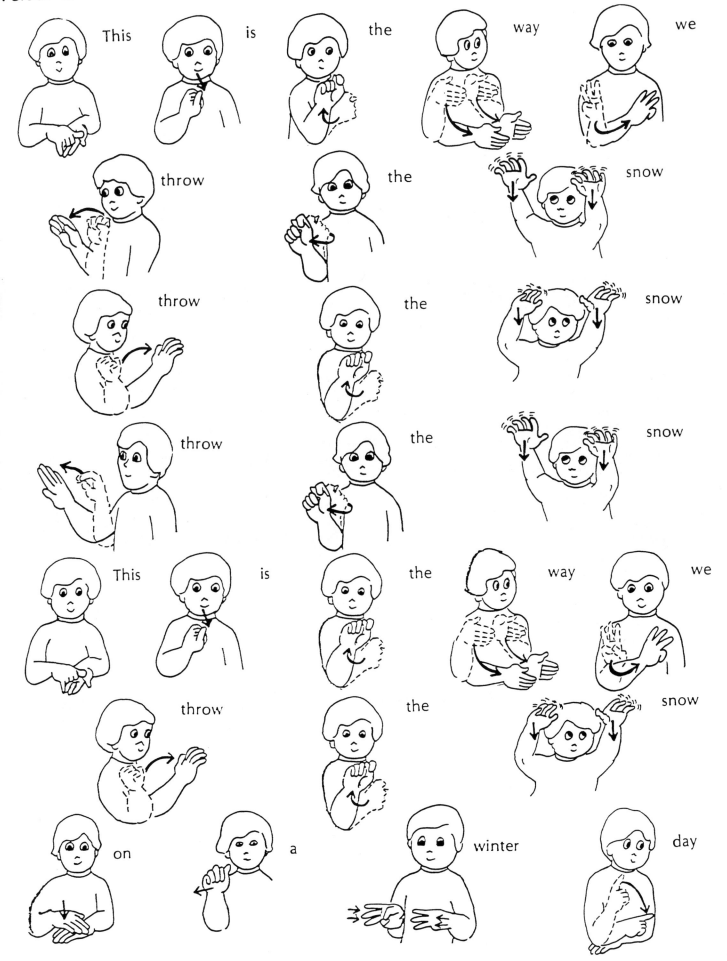

This   is   the   way   we

throw   the   snow

throw   the   snow

throw   the   snow

This   is   the   way   we

throw   the   snow

on   a   winter   day

Sing Your Way Home

Smile ev - 'ry mile, for wher -

ev - er you roam It will bright - en

your road, It will light - en your

55

load,   If   you   sing   your   way   home.

Riddle Song

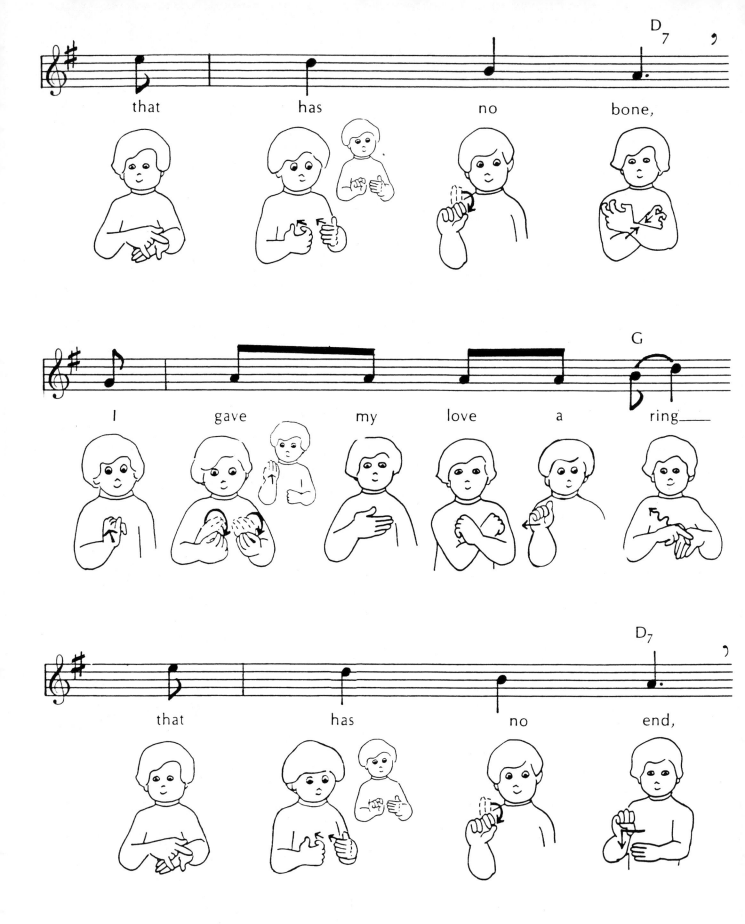

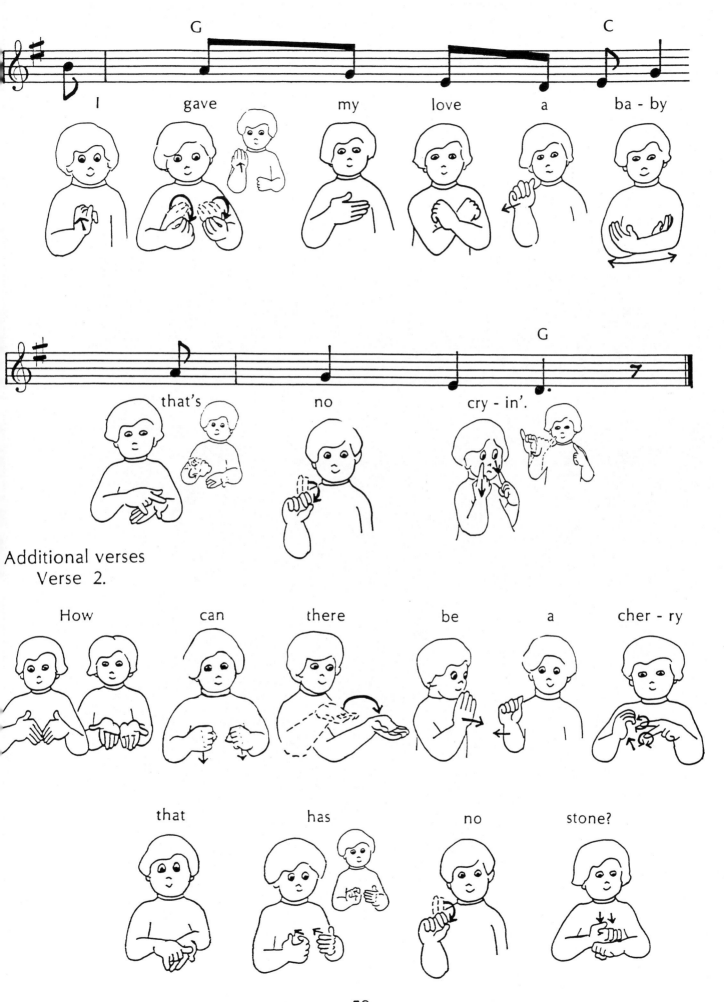

Additional verses
Verse 2.

How   can   there   be   a

chick-en   that   has   no   bone?

How   can   there   be   a

ring____   that   has   no   end?

How   can   there   be   a   ba - by

that's   no   cry - in'?

Verse 3.

A   cher - ry   when   it's   bloom-ing

it   has   no   stone,

A   chick - en   when   it's   pipp - in'

it   has   no   bone,

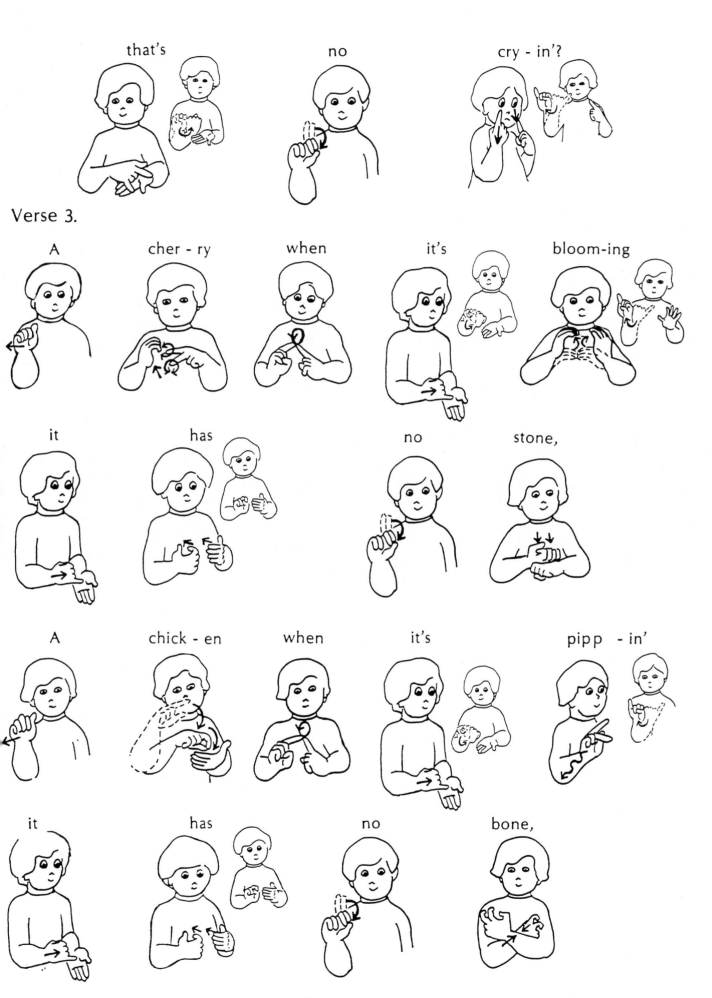

61

A   ring   when   it's   a - roll - in'

it   has   no   end,

A   ba - by   when   it's   sleep'in'

is   no   cry - in'.

Turn! Turn! Turn!

(To Everything There Is A Season)
Words from the Book of Ecclesiastes. Adaptation and Music by Pete Seeger

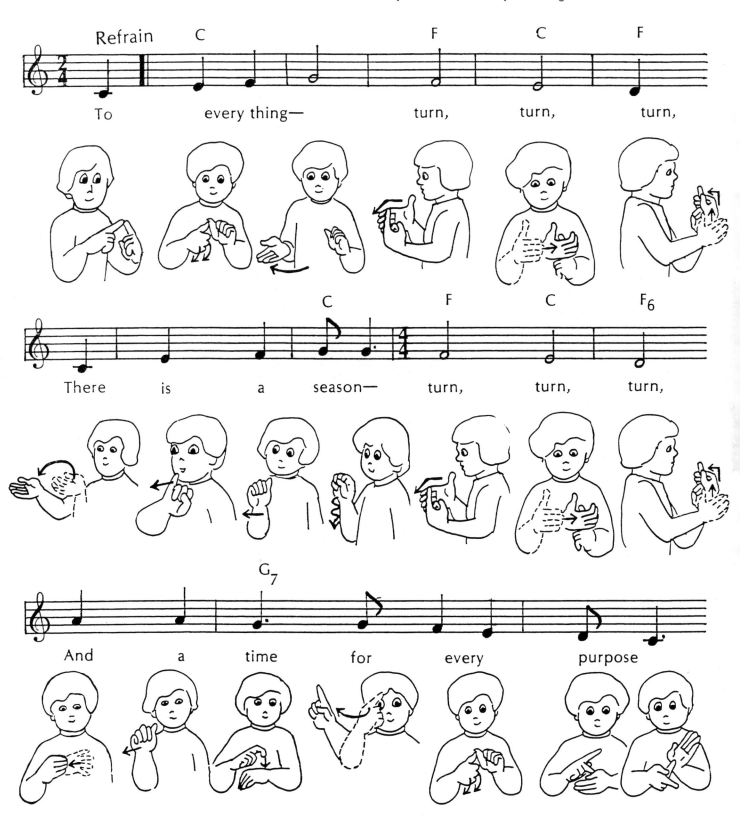

day,   A   time   to   sleep,   a   time   to

wake,   a   time   for   candles

on   the   cake.   to

Repeat Refrain

VERSE 2

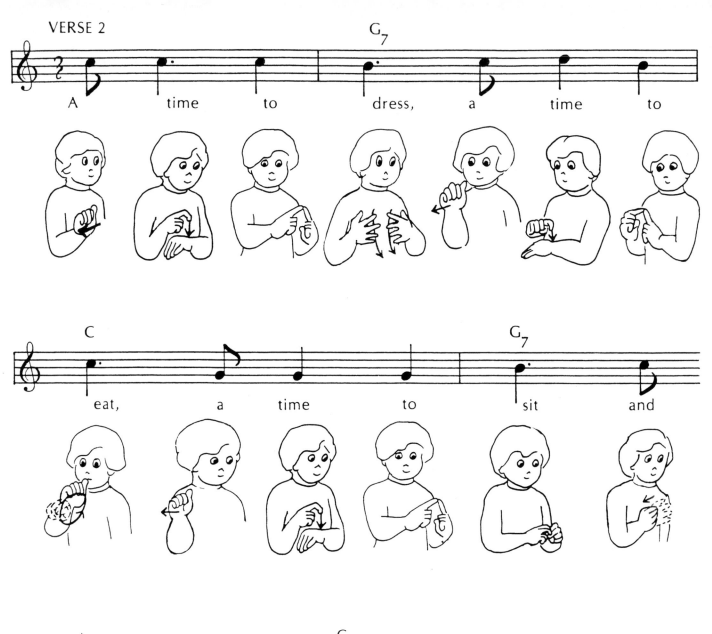

A   time   to   dress,   a   time   to

eat,   a   time   to   sit   and

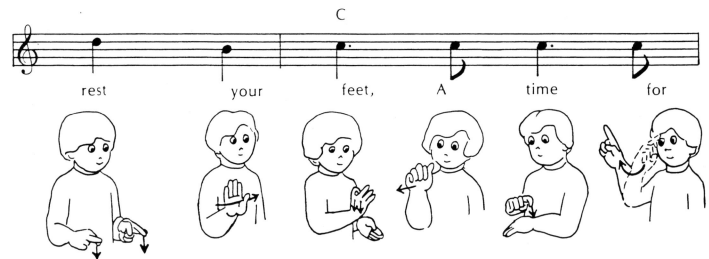

rest   your   feet,   A   time   for

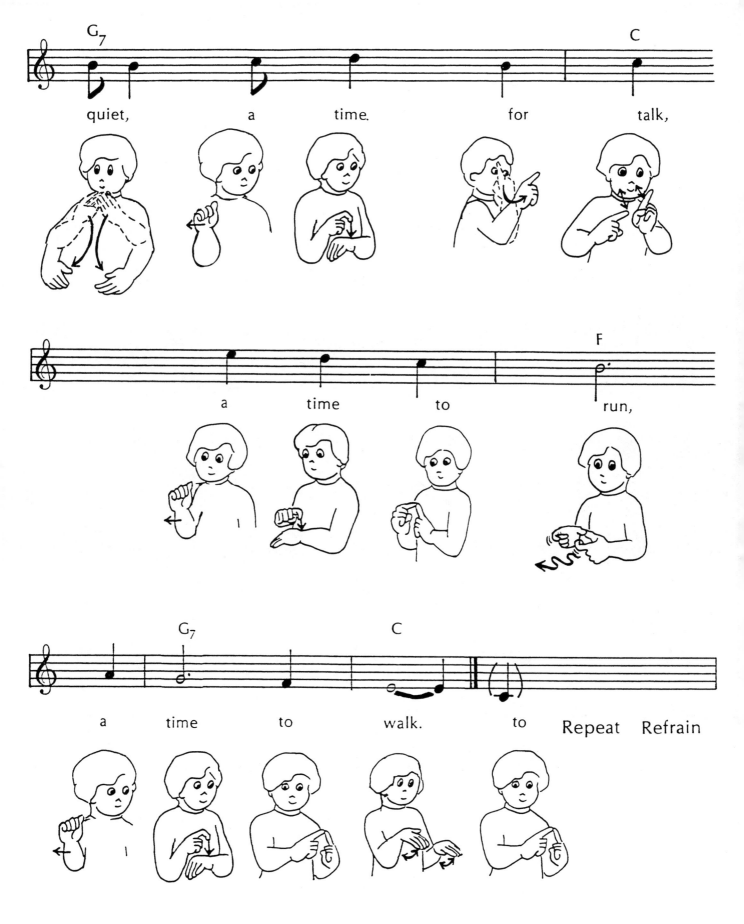

quiet,   a   time.   for   talk,

a   time   to   run,

a   time   to   walk.   to   Repeat Refrain

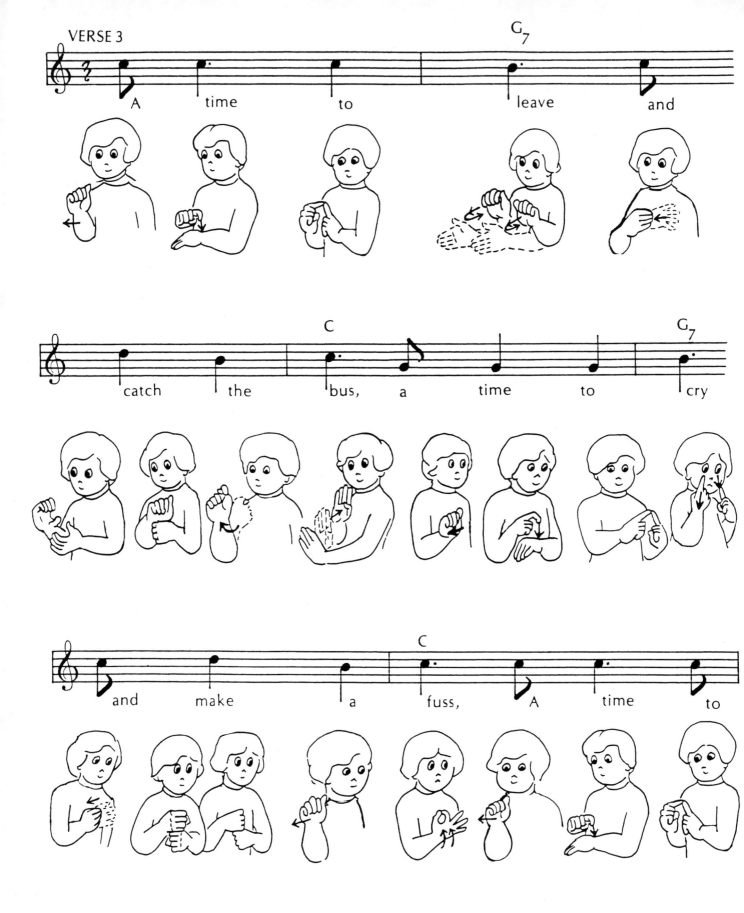

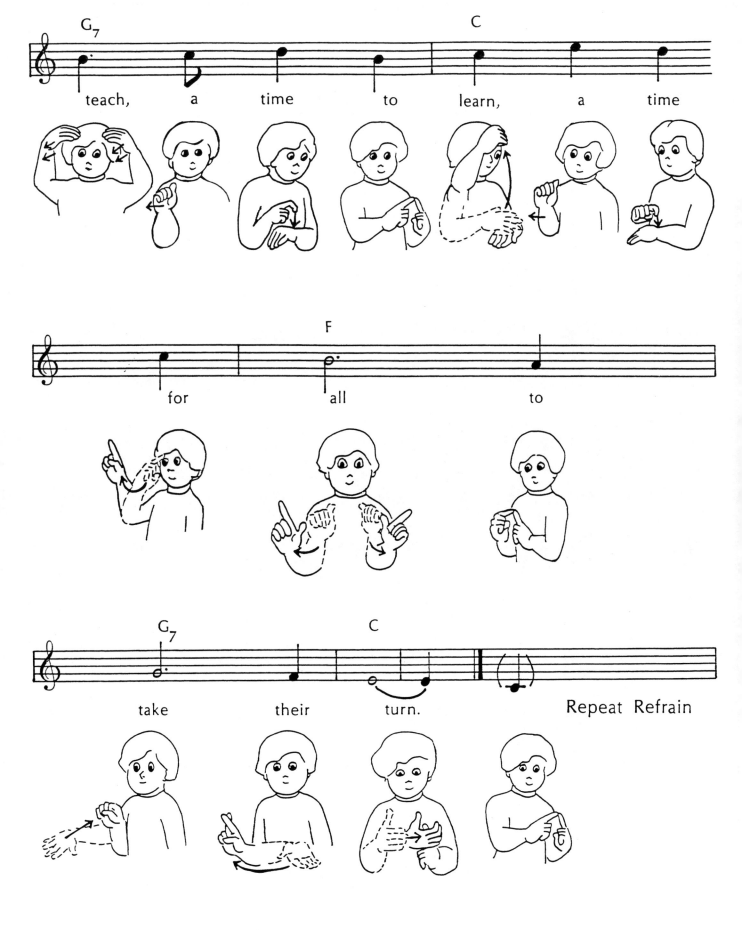

teach,   a   time   to   learn,   a   time

for   all   to

take   their   turn.   Repeat Refrain

69

Tomorrow

lyric by Martin Charnin: music by Charles Strouse from "Annie"

F maj7   Bb maj 7

a - bout____   to - mor - row   clears   a-way   the

A m7   D m

cob-webs   and   the   sor-row____   till

Bb maj 7   C sus

there's   none.   When   I'm

come what may! To - mor - row, to - mor - row, I

love ya to - mor - row, you're

al - ways
on - ly

a day a - way!

74

The mor-row, to-mor-row, I love ya to-mor-row,

you're al-ways a day a-way!
on-ly

To-mor-row, to-mor-row, I love ya to-mor-row,

you're   al - ways   a   day   a - way!____
on - ly

This Land Is Your Land

Words and Music by Woody Guthrie

Sing 1st verse as refrain after each verse.

C

This   land   is   your   land,____

G

this   land   is   my   land,____

D7   G

From   Cal - i - for nia__   to   the   New York   is - land,____

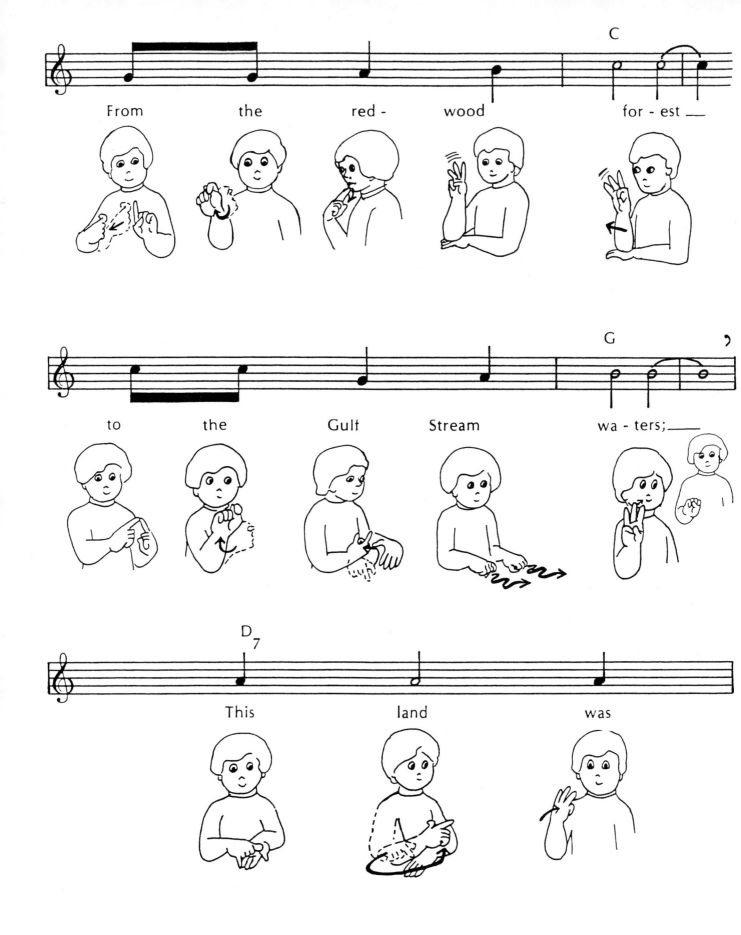

made   for   you   and   me.____

Additional verses

Verse 2.   As   I   was   walking

that   ribbon   of   highway,

I   saw   above   me

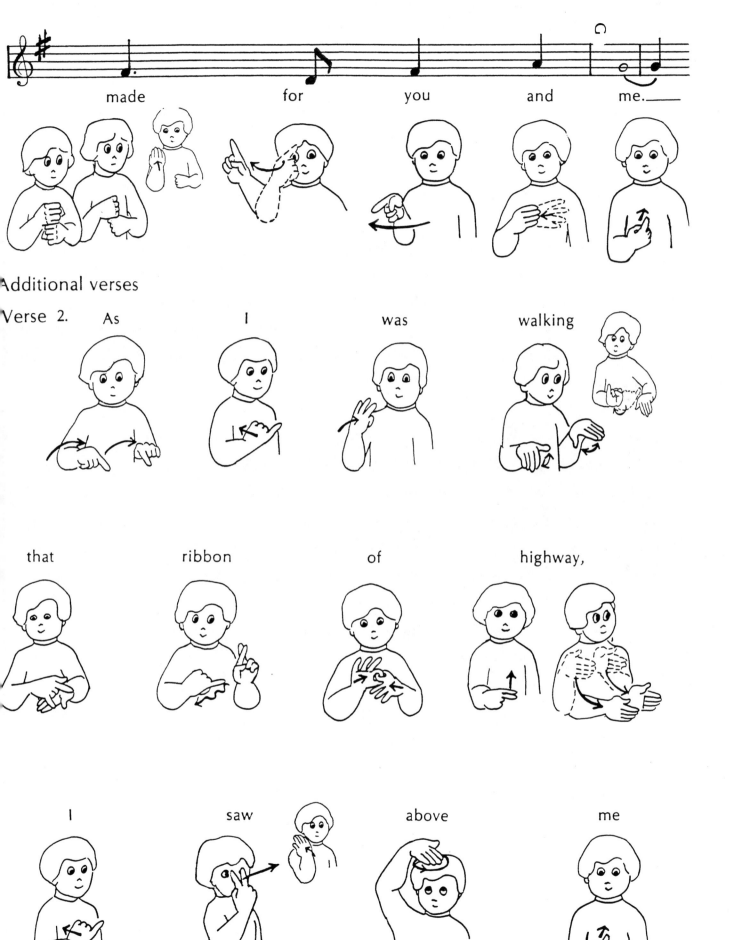

that endless skyway,

I saw below me

that golden valley;

This land was made

for you and me.

Repeat Refrain

Verse 3.

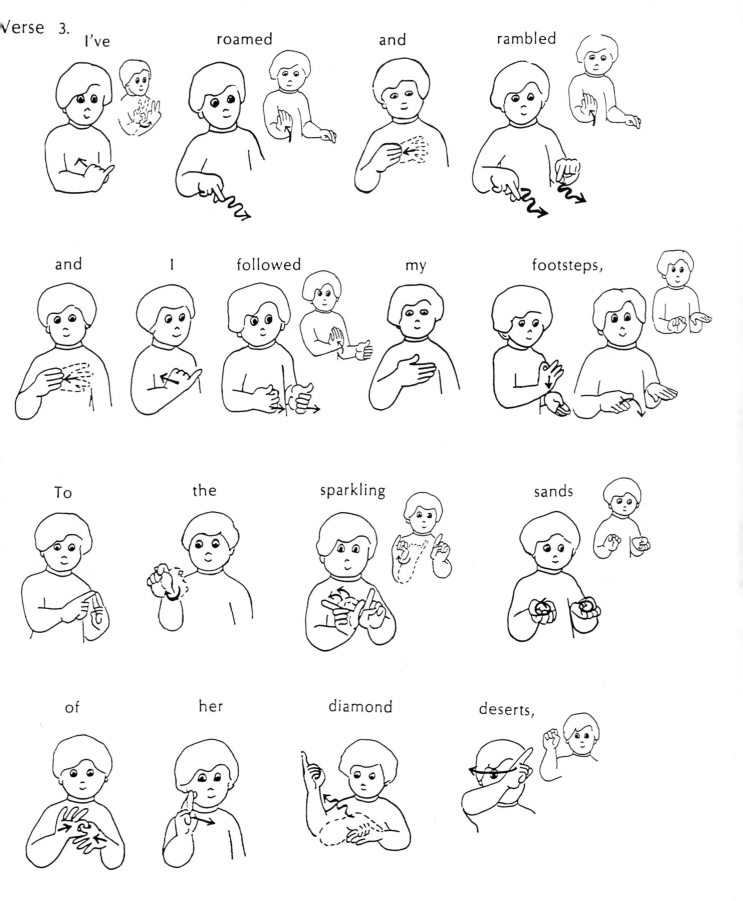

I've   roamed   and   rambled

and   I   followed   my   footsteps,

To   the   sparkling   sands

of   her   diamond   deserts,

And all around me

a voice came sounding,

This land was made

for you and me.

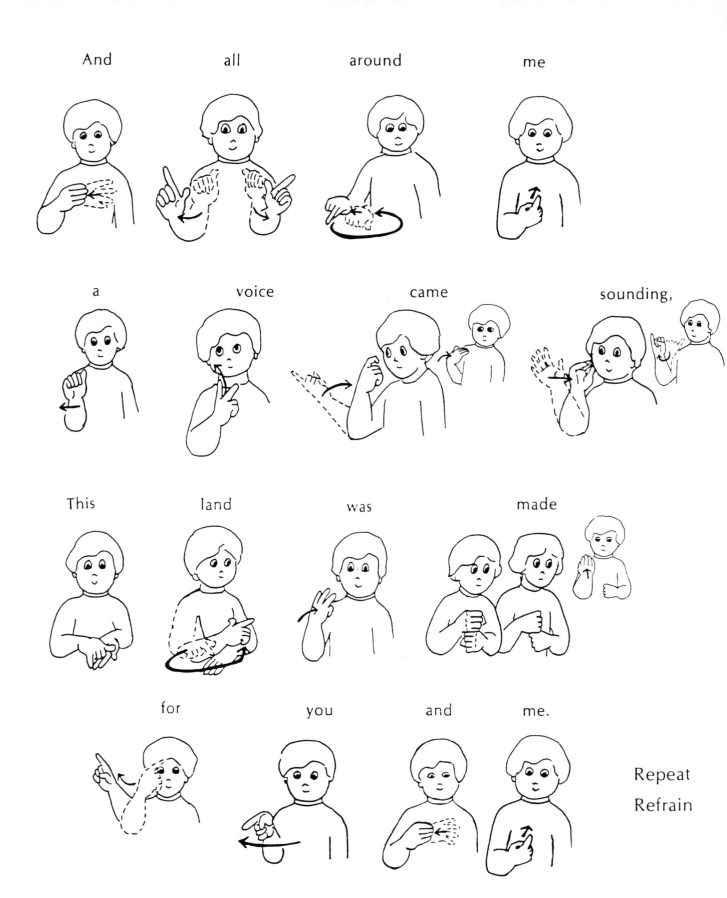

Repeat
Refrain

Rudolph The Red-Nosed Reindeer

Words and Music by Johnny Marks

Ru-dolph, the red - nosed rein - deer

had a ver - y shin - y nose,

and if you ev - er saw it,

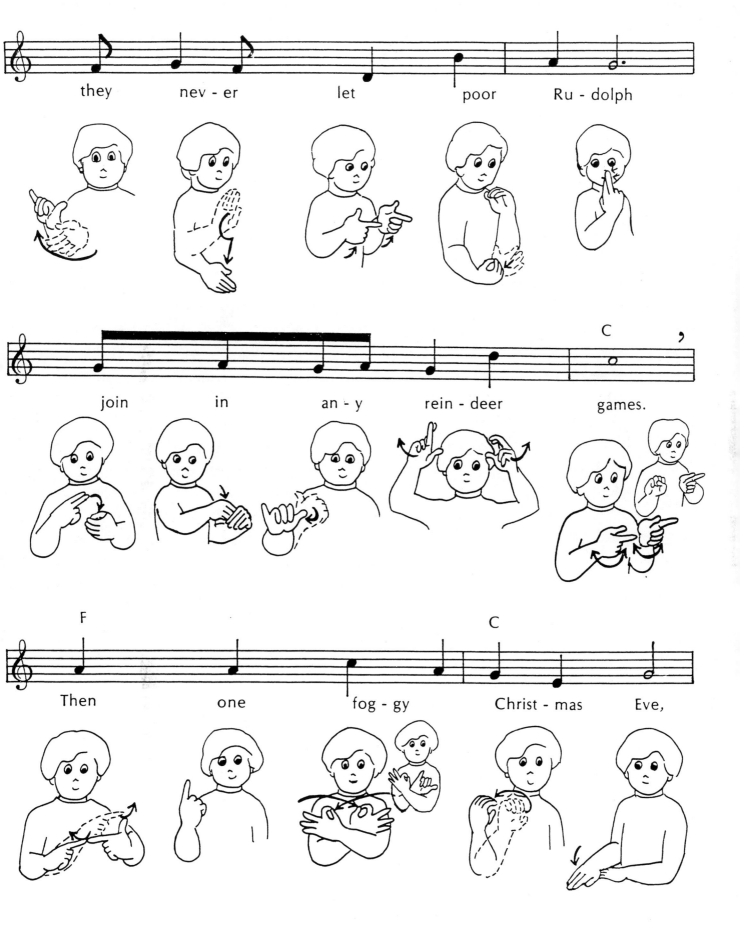

they nev - er let poor Ru - dolph

join in an - y rein - deer games.

Then one fog - gy Christ - mas Eve,

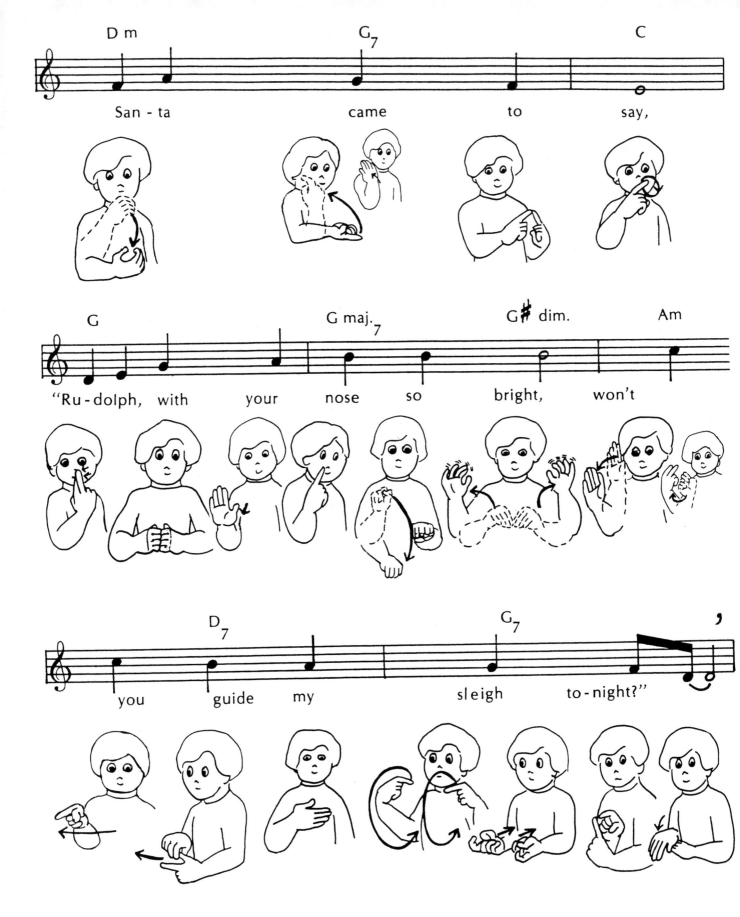

you'll   go   down   in   his - to - ry!"

you'll go down in his - to - ry!"

A Pumpkin Man

from THE SMALL SINGER by Lucille Wood and Roberta McLaughlin

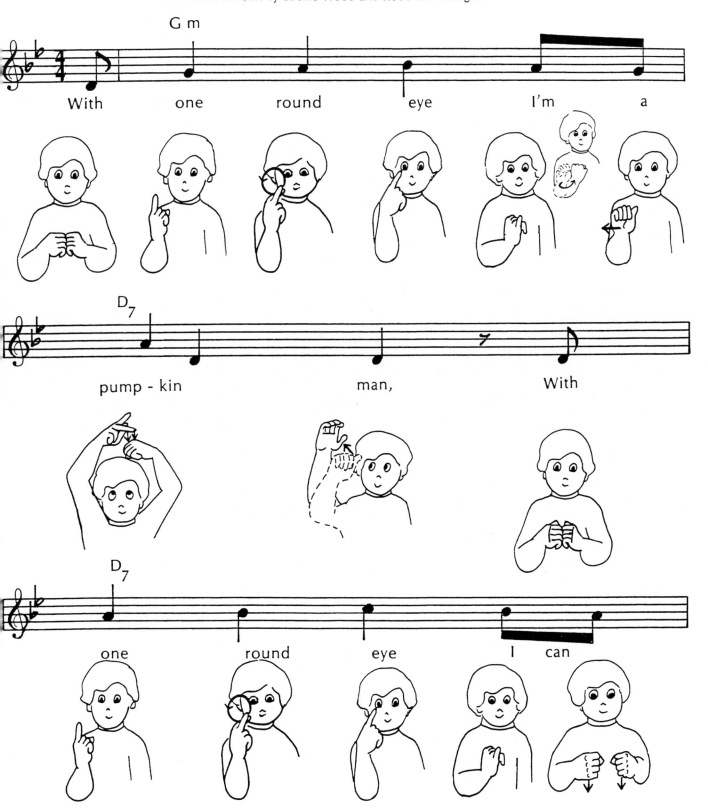

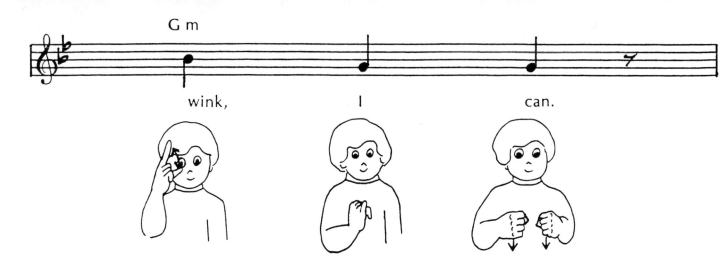

wink,   I   can.

Additional verses
Verse 2.

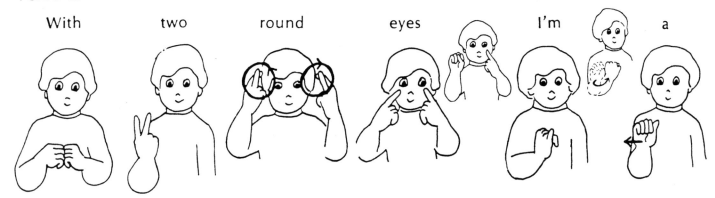

With   two   round   eyes   I'm   a

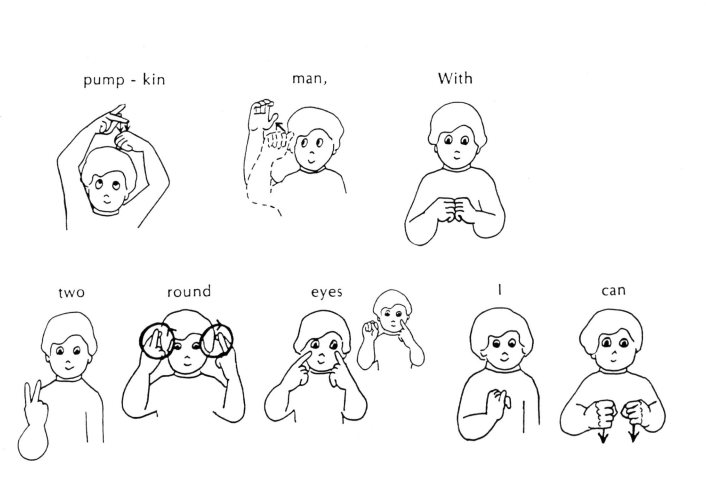

pump - kin   man,   With

two   round   eyes   I   can

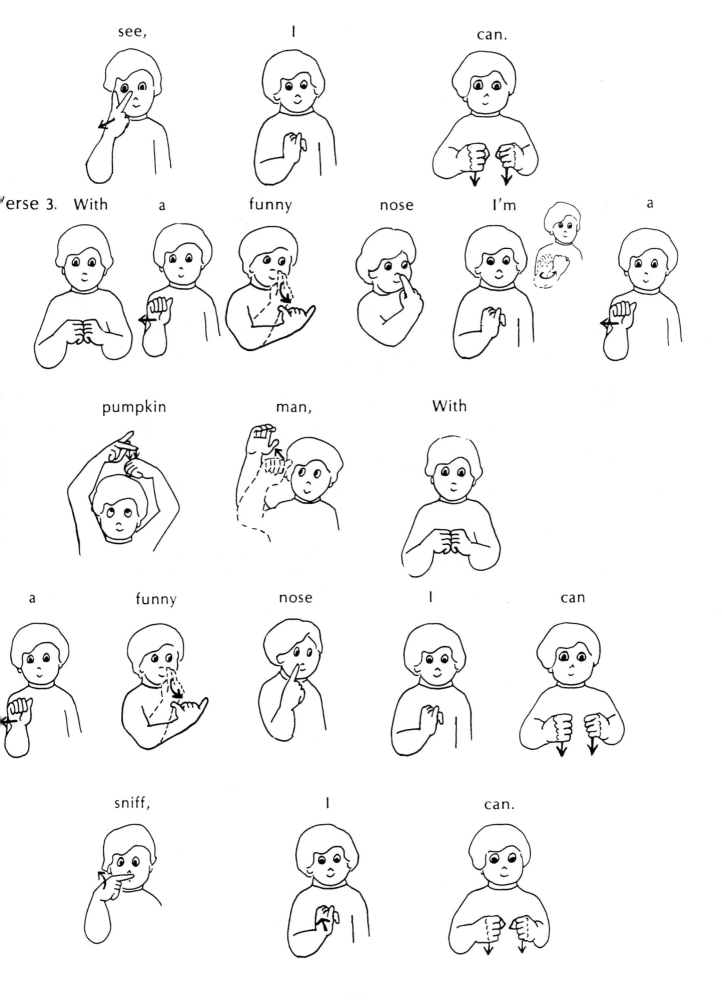

see, I can.

Verse 3. With a funny nose I'm a

pumpkin man, With

a funny nose I can

sniff, I can.

91

Verse 4.

With   a   curvy   mouth   I'm   a

pumpkin   man,   With

a   curvy   mouth   I   can

smile,   I   can.

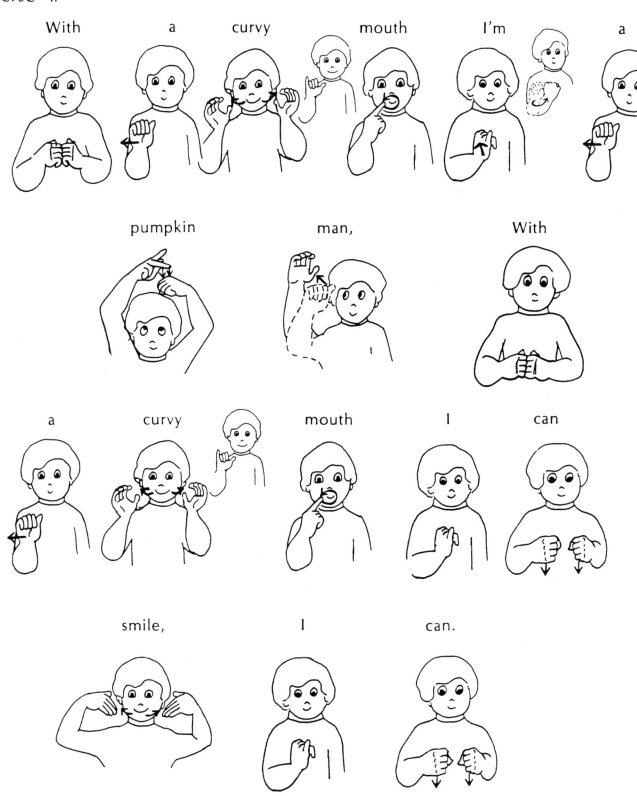

With   a   candle   light   I'm

pumpkin   man,   With

a   candle   light   I   can

shine,   I   can.

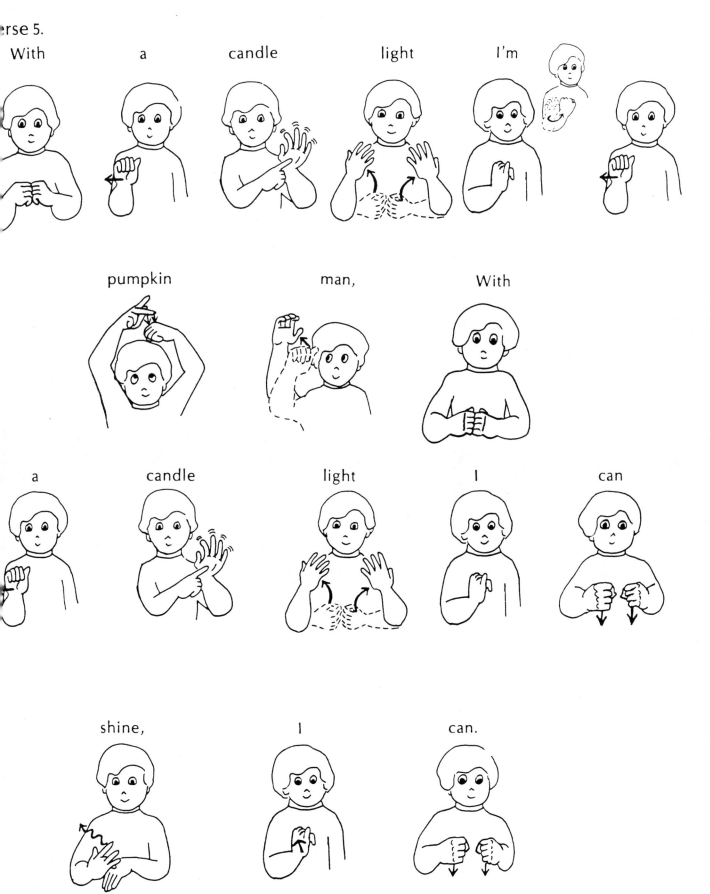

Easter Rabbit

from THE SMALL SINGER by Lucille Wood and Roberta McLaughlin

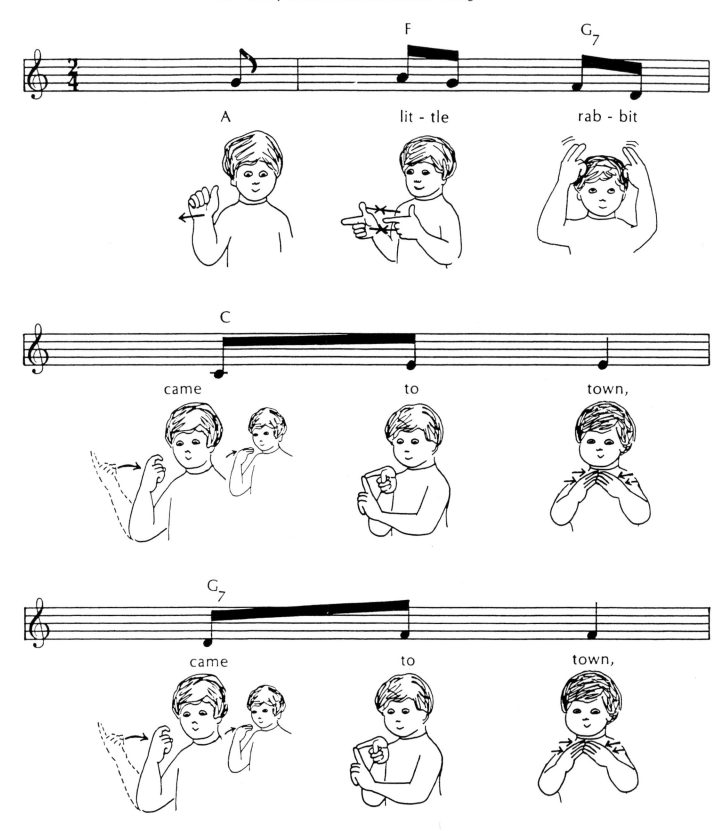

came to town. A

lit - tle rab - bit came to town,

Hop, hop, hop.

He   carried   a   bas - ket

in   his   hand,   in   his   hand,

in   his   hand.

He   carried   a   bas - ket

in   his   hand,   Hop,   hop,   hop.

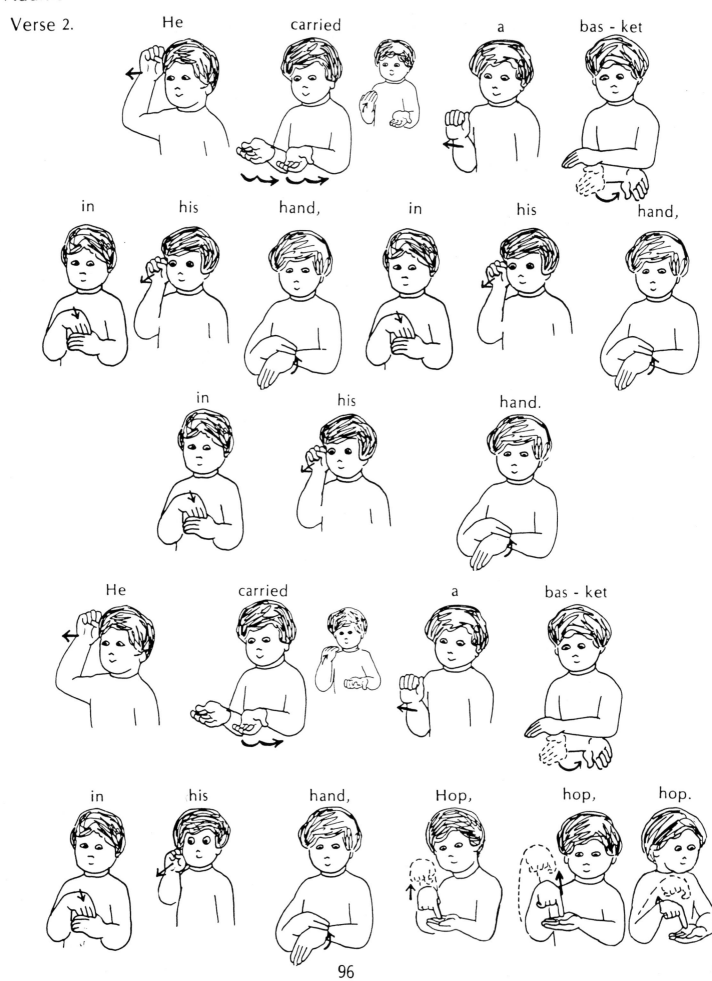

We   followed   him

around   the   town,   'round   the   town,

'round   the   town.

We   followed   him

around   the   town,   Hop,   hop,   hop.

Verse 4.

The   little   rabbit

hid   his   eggs,   hid   his

eggs,   hid   his   eggs.

The   little   rabbit   hid   his

eggs,   Hop,   hop,   hop.

98

On　　　　　Easter　　　　　Day　　　　　we

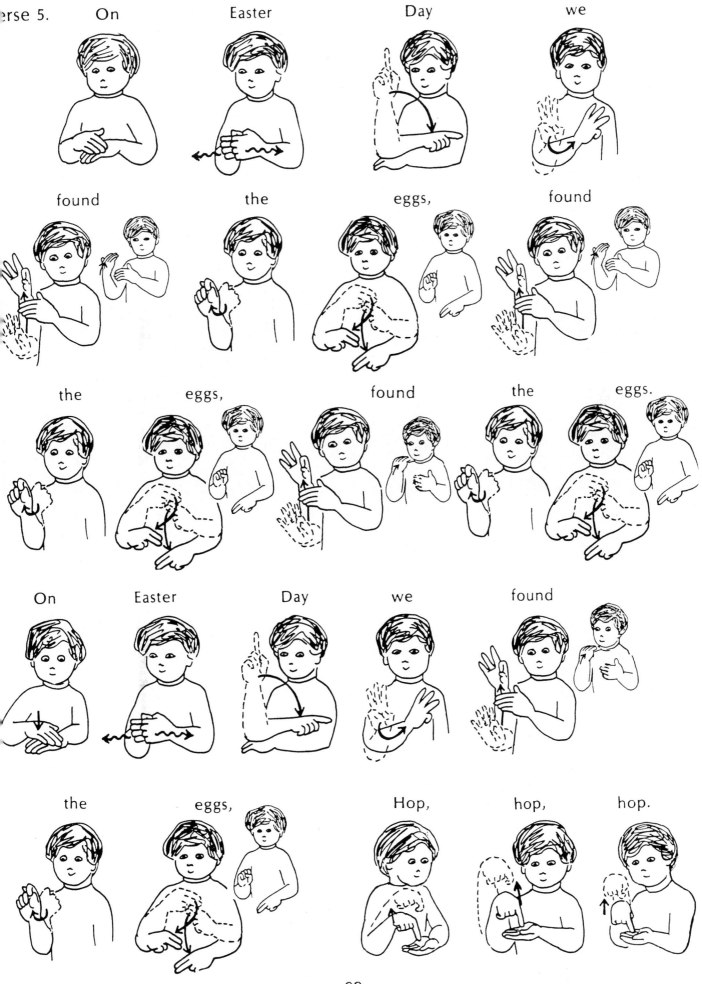

found　　　　　the　　　　　eggs,　　　　　found

the　　　　　eggs,　　　　　found　　　　　the　　　　　eggs.

On　　　Easter　　　Day　　　we　　　found

the　　　　　eggs,　　　　　Hop,　　　hop,　　　hop.

99

Verse 6. We thank you for the

Easter eggs, Easter eggs,

Easter eggs. We thank you

for the Easter eggs,

Hop, hop, hop.

100

GLOSSARY

A	Palm-out A moves slightly right	**BLUE**	Palm-left B shakes from wrist
ABOVE	Palm circles once over head	**BODY**	Touch chest and then ribs
AGAIN	Strike heel of left hand with bent right fingertips	**BONE**	Bent-3's palm-in, wrists tap against each other
AGES	A circles, then touches left palm, sign-S	**BOTTOM**	Right fingertips tap heel of palm-out left B
AIR	A-hands sweep from side to side twisting at wrists	**BRIGHT**	Flat-O's together change to 5-hands, palm-out; separate upwards with fluttering fingers
ALL	Palm-out A slides right, changing to L	**BRIGHTEN**	Sign "Bright," then flat hands twist from palms facing to palms down
ALONG	Heel of A slides up left arm to elbow		
AN	Palm-up A twists to palm-down	**BUS**	Left B, palm-right, in from of right B, palm-left; right moves back
AND	Palm-in, 5-hand pulls to right closing to a flat-O		
ALWAYS	Palm-up index, pointing forward, circles clockwise	**BY**	Palm of right hand brushes by side of vertical, palm-right left hand
ANY	Palm-up A twists to palm-down A, changes to Y	**CAKE**	Fingertips of right claw-hand bounce on back of left hand
ARE	R, just below lips, moves forward	**CALIFORNIA**	L-Y hand wiggles down from ear to Y
AROUND	Palm-down A moves slightly right, changes to palm-down R and circles once, horizontally	**CALL**	Thumb of right C (palm-left) touches corner of mouth; hand moves short distance forward
AS	Parallel indexes at right arc up and then drop, to the left	**CAME**	"Come" + flat hand flips backwards
AT	Right fingertips approach and touch back of left fingers	**CAN**	S-hands face each other, drop sharply downwards a short way
AUTUMN'S	Right A brushes off left elbow Palm-out S twists inward	**CANDLES**	Palm of left 5 on tip of right index finger; flutter fingers
AWAY	Palm-in hand flips forward and up to palm-down	**CARES**	Right V-hand on left V-hand, circle horizontally, add S-hand
BABY	Rock baby		
BACK	Extended-A thumb jerks back over shoulder	**CARRY**	Palms-up, move to side in small vertical arcs
BASKET	Flat hand draws basket under left arm	**CARRIED**	"Carry," then flip flat hand backwards
BE	B below lips; move forward	**CATCH**	Palm-out claw above side of left claw; right drops onto left; both close to S's
BEHIND	B behind A-hand turns to A and arcs to rest against left A-wrist		
BELOW	B drops to L, which falls slightly	**CHERRY**	Twist C first around left hand's upper V-finger, then around lower finger
BET	Palm-up hands, right behind left, move forward-left and turn palm-down	**CHICKEN**	G drops from mouth to close on left palm
BIRDS	Close finger on thumb twice, hand at chin, add S-hand	**CHIN**	Index finger circles slightly on chin
BIRTHDAY	Palm-up hands move from sides forward, to rest right on left. Right 1-hand drops down on left arm	**CHRISTMAS**	Twist C inward
		CLEAR	Flat-O's touching open to 5-hands
BLOOMING	Flat-O's together change to 5's with thumbs touching. I-hand twists to right, ending palm-out	**CLOSE**	Palms down, flat hands close, sides meeting
BLOWS	Palm-in flat-O at mouth moves out and opens to palm-in 5; hits side of index finger, add S-hand	**CLOUD**	C-hands face each other above eyes; move right

COBWEBS	C-hand, then place right W on back of left W, palms down, add S-hand
COLD	S's shake as if shivering
COLOR	Fingers flutter in front of chin
COMES	Palm-up index points out; beckons once, add S-hand
CORNERS	Flat hands tap fingertips in corner shape. add S-hand
COVERS	Curved palm-up covers left S-hand, add S-hand
CRY	Drag index fingers alternately down cheeks, marking tear-tracks
CRYING	Add I-hand, twisting to palm-out
CURVY	Palm-out C curves downward, add Y-hand
CUT	V-fingers snip off end of middle fingertip of flat left hand
DANCING	Palm-in V-fingertips arc from side to side, brushing left palm. Add I-hand, twisting to palm-out
DAY	Right 1-hand drops down on left arm
DEAR	D-hands cross on heart
DEEDS	Palm-down D-hands move side to side
DESERTS	D moves across forehead to right
DIAMOND	D rises shaking from left ring-finger
DID	Palm-down C-hands move side to side. Flip flat hand backwards, palm-in
DOG	Fingers of D-hand snap several times
DOLLAR	Flat-O grasps end of horizontal hand, then slips off; repeat
DON'T	Palm-down C-hands move side to side, then palm-out N twists inward
DOWN	Palm-in hand moves down
DRESS	Thumbs of palm-in 5-hands brush down chest twice
DRIVE	S-hands grasp invisible wheel, then steer
DROP	Flat-O drops and opens (can be done with 2 hands)
DROPS	Sign "Drop" and add S-hand
EARS	Point to ears plus S-hand
EARTH	Thumb and middle finger hold sides of left S; right hand rocks back and forth as on axis
EASTER	Palm-to-palm E-hands separate, shaking
EAT	Extended-A circles in and up near mouth spooning food in
EDEN	Right E-hand passes above head under left E-hand
EGGS	Right H breaks on the left H, add S-hand
END	Palm-out E slides along side of left hand and down fingertips
ENDLESS	Sign "End" then drop right bent hand down from under left bent hand
ETERNITY	Palm-out E circles and moves forward, thumb of Y-hand slides down left palm
EVE	Flat right hand "sets" over left to a level position
EVEN	E-fingertips touch, and then N-fingertips
EVER	Palm-out E circles
EVERY	Thumbtip of right A slides twice down thumb of left A
EVERYBODY	Sign "Every," then touch chest, then ribs
EVERYTHING	Sign "Every," then palm-up, arc right hand slightly up and down to the right
EYE	Point to eye
EYES	Sign "Eye" with both hands and add S-hand
FALLING	Palm-down V on elbow twists over and out to palm-up. I-hand twists to palm-out
FAR	A-hands together, right arcs forward
FAST	Indexes point forward, one ahead of the other, jerk back to X's
FEET	F-hand moves down past flat left wrist twice
FIND	F-hand pulls up past palm of left hand
FISH	Hand flutters forward like swimming
FIVE	Hold up 5 fingers, palm-in
FLAME	Palm-in F moves up, flutters fingers
FLOOR	Palm-down flat hands separate
FLY	Bent hands at shoulders flap fingers like wings
FOGGY	From sides, arc up and cross palm-in F's at wrists. Add Y-hand
FOLLOWED	Right A follows left A; both move forward left; flip flat hand backwards
FOOT	F-hand moves down past flat left wrist
FOR	Index on forehead twists to palm-out

FOREST	Elbow of F on back of left hand, shake F slightly to right	**HAD**	Sign "Have" + flip flat hand backwards
FOUND	F-hand pulls up past palm of left hand and flip palm back towards shoulder	**HAS**	Sign "Have," and add S-hand
		HAT	Pat head
FOUR	Hold up four fingers, palm in	**HAVE**	Fingertips of slightly bent hands approach and touch chest
FREE	Palm-in F's, crossed at wrists, separate and twist to palm-out	**HE**	E at temple moves forward, slightly right
FREEDOM	Sign "Free," then D on back of hand circles out left, and back along left arm	**HEAVEN**	Right flat hand passes above head under left hand and up (entering heaven)
FROM	Back of palm-in X touches palm-out left index, then moves toward body	**HER**	Palm-out R slides down jawline forward
FUNNY	Palm-in U on nose strokes downward to palm-in N. Add Y	**HID**	Sign "Hide," then flip flat hand backwards
FUSS	Palm-in F taps on chest sharply	**HIDE**	A at chin moves down under bent hand, top of thumb against left palm
GAMES	G-hands, one palm-out, one palm-in, swing back and forth, pivoting at wrists	**HIGH**	H hand moves upward
		HIGHWAY	"High" + "Way"
GET	Right open hand above left, draw both toward body, closing to S-hands	**HIM**	M at temple moves forward and slightly right
GAVE	Palm-in flat-O's near body turn outwards to palm-up, flip flat hand backwards	**HIS**	S at forehead moves forward and slightly right
GLAD	G-hand brushes chest upward; repeat	**HISTORY**	H circles forward from right shoulder
GLEE	Side of G-hand brushes up chest	**HOLD**	Right claw-hand seizes left index finger
GLOWS	G-thumb and finger on back of left hand; raise hand up and off, shaking	**HOME**	Flat-O fingertips on chin then flat palm on cheek
GO	G-hands face each other, roll out to point forward	**HOP**	Index fingertip on left palm hops up to X several times
GOT	Sign "Get" and flip flat hand backwards	**HOW**	Backs of palm-down bent hands touching, roll hands from inward to outward
GOLDEN	G at ear shakes downward to right	**HUMBLE**	Right B-hand, palm-left, moves down under left palm-down hand
GONE	"Go" plus hands from flat palms facing to palms down	**I**	Palm-left I-hand touches chest
GRAINS	G brushes up twice through left C-hand	**IF**	I-hand; two middle fingers move up into a F-hand; may repeat
GRAY	Side of G moves right across forehead	**I'M**	Sign "I," then M twisting to palm-in
GREEN	Palm-left G shakes	**IN**	Fingertips of right flat-O enter left O
GRIN	G-hands twist upwards near corners of mouth	**IS**	I on chin moves straight forward
GUIDE	Right hand grasps G-thumb and pulls left hand toward right	**ISLAND**	Side of I circles on back of left S
		IT	Tip of I touches palm of left hand
GULF	Palm-out to palm-in G outlines curves of left palm from index to thumb	**IT'S**	Sign "It," plus S-hand twisting inward
		I'VE	Sign "I," plus V-hand twisting to palm-in
HAND	H-finger draws across back of left hand	**JOIN**	H-fingertips arc into side of left O
HANG	Hook right X on side of left H	**JUST**	I-fingertip draws "J" on left palm
HAPPY	Open hand brushes middle of chest upward; repeat	**KINDNESS**	K-hands circle vertically around each other, stopping one on top of the other

KNOCKING	Right S-hand knocks several times on left palm; I-hand twists to palm-out
LAND	L on back of left hand circles out, back to elbow and along arm to hand
LAUGH	Index fingers of L's brush up and outward at corners of mouth several times
LEARN	Open palm-down fingers on palm-up left hand rise, closing to flat-O at forehead
LEFT (past tense	Flat palms face each other at side, pointing slightly up; drop down to point forward, then withdraw back and up, closing to palm-down A's, flip palm backwards over shoulder
LEGS	Hands pat thighs; add S-hand
LEND	Right V on left V, arc both forward
LESS	Bent hand under other bent hand; right hand drops downward
LET	L-hands face each other, pointing down; swing to point forward
LET'S	Sign "Let," and twist S-hand to palm-in
LIGHT	Palm-in O-hands touch and open to palm-in 5-hands while moving upward
LIGHTEN	Sign "Light"; palms, facing, then drop to palms down
LIKE	Palm-in L on chest moves forward closing thumb and finger
LISTEN	Thumb of palm-out L points to ear
LITTLE	L-hands face each other, jerk slightly toward each other; repeat
LIVE	Palm-in L-hands move up body
LOAD	Palm-up L flips to palm-down on left palm-down L
LOBSTER	Palm-down V-hands, crossed at wrists, move forward and to right while V's scissor
LONE	Palm-in L moves forward
LONG	Index finger slides up left arm
LOVE	S-hands cross on heart
LOVED	Sign "Love," add flip of palm backwards
LOVELY	Palm-in L circles face
MADE	Side of S touches on side of S; both twist to palm-in and touch again; flip palm backwards
MAGIC	S's, palm-down at eye-level, open to 5's and close
MAKE	Side of S touches on side of S; both twist to palm-in and touch again

MAN	Extended-A on temple, then measure height with bent hand
MANY	Palm-up S's spring open into 5's; repeat
MAY (verb)	Palm-up flat hands move alternately up and down
ME	Index points to and touches chest
MIGHTY	M-fingertips draw muscle on left arm. Add Y
MILE	M brushes up left arm
MOMENTS	Side of M on left palm, twists to point downward. Add S
MORE	Palm-in flat O's bounce tips together twice
MOUTH	Index circles mouth once
MY	Flat hand palm on chest
NAME	Right H taps on left H twice at right angles
NAMES	Sign "Name," plus S-hand
NAME-SIGN	Tap the left shoulder with the right hand in the letter of the first letter of the desired name—"L" for Linda, "C," for Craig, etc.
NEVER	Tip of open hand draws large question-mark arc
NEW YORK	Palm-down Y slides off left palm
OCEAN	Palm-down O's move wavelike up and down forward, opening to 5's
OF	Open hands approach and link thumbs and index fingers of 9's
OH	Spell O-H with both hands
ON	Right palm touches back of left hand
ONE	Hold up index finger, palm-in
ONLY	Palm-out index twists to palm-in
OR	Palm-out O off left L-thumb, then off fingertip
ORANGE	S squeezes in front of chin; repeat
OTHER	Palm-down A-hand; twist over to palm up
OUR	O, on right side of chest, circles to left side
OUT	Right O-hand pulls out from palm-left C
OVER	Palm-down right hand circles over back of left
PANE	Right palm-in P drops on left P twice
PENNY	Middle finger of P taps temple, moves out, then shakes
PINK	Middle finger of P brushes twice down chin

PIPPING	P outlines a crack in the egg, and I-hand twists to palm-out	**ROUND**	Palm-out R circles once
PLACE	P-tips touch ahead of you, circle, then touch nearer you	**RUN**	Palm-down L-thumbtips touch; hands move forward, index fingers flicking in and out rapidly
PLAY	Y-hands face each other; shake	**SAME**	Palm-down fingers touch sides together
PLEASANT	Palm rubs on chest in circle then the side of T slides down left palm	**SAND**	S-palms up; rub thumbs across back of fingers
POOR	Grasp left elbow; close to flat-O; repeat	**SANTA CLAUS**	Palm-in C at chin curves down to touch chest, palm-up
PUMPKIN	Middle finger of P taps on back of left S	**SAY**	Index circles up and outward near mouth
PURPLE	P shakes from wrist	**SAW**	Palm-in V from eye outward, then flip flat hand backwards, palm-in (See "SEE")
PURPOSE	P on left palm, twist and touch again		
QUIET	Flat hands cross under chin and separate downwards	**SEA**	Palm-down S's sweep up and down forward, opening to 5's
RABBIT	Palm-in U-fingers at temples wiggle backward together	**SEASONS**	Palm-out S moves downward with a wavy motion
RAIN	Palm-down claw-hands drop sharply; repeat	**SEE**	Palm-in V from eye outward
		SEVEN	Palm-out, thumb holds third finger down
RAINBOW	Sign "Rain," then palm-in S-hands arc out to V's	**SHADOWS**	Both palm-out S-hands fall and cross at wrists, add W-hand and S-hand
RAMBLED	Both R's, pointing down, move forward in a wavy path then flip flat palm backwards	**SHINE**	Bent middle finger rises off back of left hand, shaking
RED	Palm-in, index finger touches chin, brushes down and closes	**SHINY**	Sign "Shine," then LY-hand wiggles downward
REDWOOD	"Red" + Elbow of W on back of left hand; twist W slightly side to side	**SHORT**	Side of right H rubs back and forth on side of left H
REINDEER	Thumbs of R's on temples, move out and up	**SHOUTED**	C before chin jerks up and forward, right; flat hand, palm-in, flips backwards
REST	Right R behind left; both move slightly down	**SHOVEL**	Back of right hand slides forward in palm of left hand and flips up
RIBBON	Right palm-in I wiggles away and slightly down from palm-out R		
RIDDLE	Palm-out R draws question-mark	**SING**	Palm-out hand from corner of mouth arcs forward and out, slightly to the side
RIDING	First two fingers sit on thumb of horizontal palm-right C-hand and both move forward; I-hand twists to palm-out	**SIT**	Right U sits 2 fingers on left palm-down U
		SIX	Palm-out, thumb holds little finger down
RING	R shakes away from left ring finger	**SKY**	Palm-down flat hand at left arcs to palm-up hand at right
ROAD	Palm-down R's move forward, weaving slightly side to side	**SLEIGH**	Palm-in 1-hands circle forward to palm up X-hands that pull back
ROAM	R, pointing down, moves forward in a wavy path		
ROAMED	Sign "Roam," then flip flat palm backwards	**SLEEP**	Before face, 5-hand drops to flat-O, palm-in
ROLLING	R's, palms facing, roll forward around each other alternately from chest; I-hand twists to palm-out	**SLEEPING**	Sign "Sleep," then I-hand twists to palm-out
ROOF	R's outline roof	**SLIDING**	Right palm-down hand slides down and outward over back of left hand. Then I-hand twists to palm-out

SMILE	Index-finger side of bent hands curves corners of mouth up
SNIFF	X against nose, sniff with head moving slightly up
SNOW	Hands drops slowly, palm-down, fluttering fingers
SO	Right S moves sharply down, striking side of left S in passing
SOME	Side of right hand draws small arc across left palm
SOMETHING	Some+Thing
SOMEWHERE	Some+Where
SOUNDING	Palm-out 5 moves to ear, closing to flat-O; I-hand twists to palm-out
SPARKLING	Right index flicks up along-side left index; repeat; I-hand twists to palm-out
SPEND	Back of flat-O on left palm slides off, closing to A
SPRING	Flat-O "jumps" upward through C to 5; repeat
STAR	Side of right index finger strikes upward against left index finger; left strikes upward against right
STEPS	Flat hands, palms down, one hand steps forward, add S-hand
STICK	G's close on each other
STONE	Back of S raps back of left S; repeat
STREAM	Palm-down S's ripple forward to left, up and down
STUCK	Sign "Stick" and then flip flat hand backwards
SUMMER	Palm-down X is dragged across forehead
SUN	C by eye swings up to side
SWIMMING	Palms-down, breast stroke forward; I-hand twists to palm-out
TAIL	Wrist rests on left index finger; wag hand with index extended
TAKE	5-hand draws back toward body, closing to S
TALK	Index fingers move alter-nately to and from lips
TEACH	Flat-O's pointing to temples move forward slightly; repeat
TELL	Palm-down index under chin flips out to palm-up
THANK	Palm-in open hand at chin drops to palm-up
THAT	Palm-down I-L-hand on left palm

THE	Palm-in T; twist to palm-out
THEIR	Palm-up hand at left of body sweeps right to palm-out R
THEM	Palm-up hand at left of body sweeps right to palm-out M
THEN	Index moves from off left thumb to off tip of left index
THERE	Palm-up hand arcs forward
THEY	Palm-up hand at left of body; sweep right to palm-out Y
THEY'LL	Sign "They," then palm-out L twists inward
THEY'RE	Sign "They," then palm-out R twists inward
THING	Palm-up, arc right hand slightly up and down to the right
THINGS	Sign "Thing"+ S
THIS	Palm-down Y drops on palm of left hand
THREE	Palm-in, hold up first two fingers and thumb
THROUGH	Open hand slides outward between fingers of left hand
THROW	Flat-O throws forward into 5-hand
TIGHT	Right claw on left S; twist slightly right, as if to tighten cap
TILL	Right palm-in L index arcs over to touch index of palm-in left Lp
TIME	X-index finger taps wrist
TO	Horizontal index finger approaches and touches left vertical index finger
TOMORROW	Thumb on cheek, move forward and twist to point forward
TOO	O approaches and touches left index
TOWN	Fingertips touch at left, separate; touch at right
TREASURES	Palm-up T on left palm rises to palm-down T over palm
TURN	Right palm curves around left vertical index
TWINKLE	Pinch finger and thumb together at each eye
TWO	Palm-in, hold up first two fingers
UNDER	Right A slides under left palm
UP	Palm-out U moves up
US	U at right side of chest circles to left side
USE	Heel of U-hand bounces on back of left hand
USED	Sign "Use," then the letter D

VALLEY	Beginning at sides, palms-down, draw valley	**WHO**	Thumb of L on chin; wiggle index finger
VERY	Middle fingertips of V's touch and then arc apart	**WILL**	Flat hand palm facing side of head; arc forward
VOICE	Fingertips of palm-in V move up throat and out under chin	**WINDS**	Horizontal hands swing back and forth, twisting at wrists, as wind "blows" them
WAKE	Closed G-hand at corner of eye opens to L	**WINK**	Thumb of L at eye, shut and open finger
WALK	Wrists stationary, hands flip alternately	**WINTER**	W's face each other; shake slightly
WALKING	Sign "Walk," then twist I-hand to palm-out	**WITH**	A-hands together, palm to palm
WANTS	Palms-up 5's pull back to claws toward body	**WONDER**	W circles near temple
WAS	Palm-in W moves back toward shoulder	**WON'T**	Sign "Will," then palm-out N twists inward
WATER	Index finger of palm-left W taps chin	**WORDS**	Right G-fingers rest against left index
WATERS	Sign "Water," plus S	**WORK**	Palm-out S taps back of left S; repeat
WAY	Parallel flat hands move forward, weaving slightly side to side	**WORLD**	Right W on top of left W; right circles vertically around left
WE	W on right side of chest circles to left side	**WOULD**	Palm-out W-hand at side of face moves forward to D
WHAT	Index fingertip brushes down across left fingers	**YEAR**	S rests on left S; right circles vertically around left
WHEN	Indexes touch; make a circle with right index fingertip; return tip to tip	**YELLOW**	Palm-left Y shakes
		YES	Y-hand nods
WHERE	Palm-out index shakes sideways	**YOU**	Index points at person addressed
WHEREVER	Sign "Where," then palm-out E circles	**YOU'LL**	Sign "You," then palm-out L-hand twists inward
WHILE	W-hands face each other near right shoulder, arc down and forward	**YOUR**	Flat palm moves toward person addressed
WHITE	5 on chest moves outward, closing to a flat-O	**YOU'RE**	Sign "You," then palm-out R twists inward

PRODUCTS from
MODERN SIGNS PRESS, INC.

Basic Tools and Techniques
Signing Exact English The Dictionary, the heart of the SEE system
Signing Exact English Interactive CD ROM with all Dictionary information and ability to print any of the illustrated signs individually or in phrases or sentences in a variety of sizes.
Teaching and Learning Signing Exact English
Student Workbook
Vocabulary Development Flash Cards
   Kit A
   Kit B
   Kit C

Video Tapes
Curriculum Tapes
   Beginning level – 14 lessons (workbook included)
   Rather Strange Stories (Intermediate level) - 14 tapes
SIGN WITH ME Produced at Boys Town National Research Hospital
   Building Conversation
   Building Concepts
   Positive Parenting
See Me Sing Songs and stories
The Sign for Friends David Parker
Visual Tales (available in Signed English or ASL)
   The Father, The Son and The Donkey
   Village Stew
   The Greedy Cat
   The Magic Pot
   The House That Jack Built
Signed Cartoons (available in Signed English or ASL)

Three Pigs	**Three Bears**	**Casper**	**Animal Antics**
Raggedy Ann	**Jingle Bells**	**Pup's Christmas**	**Shipshape Shapes**
Rudolph	**Cinderella**	**Numbers**	**Red Riding Hood**
Reptiles, Birds & Amphibians			

Show and Tell Stories
   Series 1 – Brown Bear, Brown Bear and This Is Me
   Series 2 _ The Very Hungry Caterpillar and Goodnight Moon
   Series 3 - Nursery Rhymes
Informational Tapes
   Deafness the Hidden Handicap
   Growing Up with SEE
Instructional Video Tapes in Spanish/English

Children's Collection
Coloring Books
   ABC's of Fingerspelling
   Sign Numbers